RADCLYFFE HALL
A CASE OF OBSCENITY?

Radclyffe Hall in 1928

RADCLYFFE HALL
A CASE OF OBSCENITY?

Vera Brittain

South Brunswick
New York: A. S. Barnes and Company

RADCLYFFE HALL A CASE OF OBSCENITY? © By Vera
Brittain 1968. First American edition published
1969 by A. S. Barnes and Company Inc., Cranbury,
New Jersey 08512.

Library of Congress Catalogue Card Number: 76-81684

SBN 498 07451 X

Printed in the United States of America

CONTENTS

ILLUSTRATIONS

CONTENTS

ILLUSTRATIONS

ACKNOWLEDGEMENTS

I wish to express my sincere thanks for the generous help and co-operation given during my research both here and in the U.S.A. by the following:

R. J. Minney, Clifford Allen, Dr Paul Gebhard, Director of the Institute for Sex Research, Indiana University, Miss Jessie B. Heard, Dr Sawle Thomas, R. Lovat Dickson, Brian Magee, Beresford Egan, Morris L. Ernst, Alan U. Schwartz, Montgomery Hyde, Alec Craig.

Also permission from the various publishing houses to quote, including:

George Allen and Unwin Ltd., Jonathan Cape Ltd., Chappell and Co. Ltd., W. B. Saunders Co. (Philadelphia).

For contemporary comment and other passages I am indebted to a number of newspapers and magazines, among them:

The Daily Express, The Daily Mirror, The Evening News, The Daily Herald, The News of the World, The Sunday Express, The Times, The New York Times, New York Herald Tribune, Brooklyn Daily Eagle, Philadelphia Enquirer, Philadelphia Public Ledger, The Nation, The New Republic, The Spectator, The New Statesman, The New Law Journal, Time and Tide, Man and Society.

Last, and by no means least, I should like to thank Paul F. Berry for his patient research on my behalf at the British Museum and my husband, Professor George Catlin, for his valuable help in New York.

AUTHOR'S FOREWORD

In November, 1928, one of the most sensational prosecutions in the history of publishing centred upon Bow Street Police Court.

The action was initiated by the Home Secretary, Sir William Joynson-Hicks (popularly known as 'Jix'), after an attack by James Douglas, the Editor of the *Sunday Express,* on August 19th, 1928, upon a novel entitled *The Well of Loneliness,* written by Radclyffe Hall and published by Jonathan Cape Limited.

Sir Chartres Biron, the Bow Street magistrate, heard the case and pronounced the book obscene. Mr Norman Birkett (as he then was) called Mr Desmond MacCarthy, Editor of *Life and Letters,* and asked him only one question: 'In your opinion is this book obscene?'

This was promptly disallowed. He asked him no other questions and Mr MacCarthy left the witness box without giving any evidence. Mr Birkett then announced that he had thirty-nine other witnesses whom he formally tendered, telling the magistrate that he intended asking them the very same question. Sir Chartres Biron would not admit their evidence and the witnesses were not called.

The following month an Appeal failed, and the magistrate ordered the book to be destroyed. It was subsequently published in France and fourteen other countries, and was eventually republished in Britain by the Grey Walls Press. This publishing house no longer exists, and its proprietor, Mr Peter Baker, died in November 1966.

As a young would-be writer beginning my career with free-lance journalism, I had reviewed the book – critically, but on the whole favourably – in *Time and Tide* for August 10th, 1928, and hence was one of the assembly of witnesses for the defence on whom silence was imposed.

I should not today review this long, emotional novel in quite the same terms, but a book, to be treated fairly, has to be reviewed within the climate of its own generation. Though hindsight would not impel me to change a good deal, I am still impressed by its passionate honesty and the author's courage in presenting her case to a hostile and intolerant public. I still feel that she had a real appreciation of beauty, shown especially in her vivid small vignettes of country scenes, and that her quality of compassion was quite exceptional.

When Femina Books was formed to publish books of definite interest to women, they asked me to contribute my recollection of this famous case. The author, publisher, magistrate and many of the witnesses are now dead, but I am happy to record my still vivid memories for a society in which the attitude of most readers to such biological phenomena as sexual inversion, and the public reaction to so-called obscenity, have changed beyond recognition in the past forty years.

Whitehall Court, S.W.1. 1968.   V.B.

INTRODUCTION
BY C. H. ROLPH

'I PROTEST, I emphatically protest!', cried Miss Radclyffe Hall, to the scandal of the decorous but crowded courtroom. She was told to be quiet: the magistrate was speaking.

'I am the author of this book!', she went on recklessly, and a few more words would have got her outside in the corridor, among the waiting drunks and the prostitutes. She was persuaded to sit down.

As the mere author of the book she was nobody. The defendant was the book – *The Well of Loneliness*. The only person who could speak in its defence was he who had been found to be keeping it in his 'house, shop, room, or other place for the purpose of sale or distribution'. That happened to be Mr Jonathan Cape, its publisher, and the manager of Pegasus Press, who printed it, and they were both in court to 'show cause why the copies seized should not be destroyed'. The whole process was logically and legally reasonable and dispassionate.

But, of course, as Hazlitt said:

> 'Women have often more of what is called good sense than men. They have fewer pretensions; are less implicated in theories; and judge of objects more from their immediate and involuntary impression on the mind and, therefore, more truly and naturally. They cannot reason wrong, for they do not reason at all.'

The whole *Well of Loneliness* tragi-comedy is such a feast of unreason that it is interesting to slip back for the necessary forty years and remind oneself what the times and manners were like.

It helps if you keep at the back of your mind the mini-skirted, flat-chested, tango-hipped puppets of those *Boy Friend* days, and the rising voices of Scott Fitzgerald, Aldous Huxley, Kafka, Virginia Woolf, Sean O'Casey and Noel Coward. You should also remember that the nineteen-twenties saw the publication – in this country – of books as uninhibited as Theodore Dreiser's *An American Tragedy*, T. E. Lawrence's *Seven Pillars of Wisdom,* Sinclair Lewis's *Elmer Gantry,* D. H. Lawrence's *Lady Chatterley's Lover* (thus to begin its long guerrilla war with the authorities), Remarque's *All Quiet on the Western Front,* and Joyce's *Ulysses*. They couldn't have been so mealy-mouthed or defenceless. Even in 1928, the year of *The Well of Loneliness,* a shocked London allowed itself to go on being shocked (paying avidly for it at the box office) by John van Druten's play *Young Woodley*. It is true that there had been a general welcome for *Winnie the Pooh, Polyanna* (Mary Pickford had just married Douglas Fairbanks), *Lilac Time* (lollipop Schubert), *Sorrel and Son, Carry on, Jeeves, Tarka the Otter,* and the first *Mickey Mouse* in colour.

Meanwhile angry people were daubing green paint on Epstein's *Rima* in Hyde Park, and the papers were full of derision and complaint about Henry Moore's new *Draped Reclining Figure*. George Grossmith's newly introduced cabaret entertainments and the rapid growth of night-clubs seemed to observers like James Douglas, of the *Sunday Express*, infinitely more menacing than the idle mills, the deserted pits, the vast processions of hunger marchers and the smouldering despair of a defeated and incredulous Germany.

It may then have seemed a sophisticated time, but as usual the sophistication touched the lives of about two per cent of the population, the other ninety-eight per cent playing out their lives on well-established lines of traditional hard work, Saturday nights, football and the boozer. As social sedatives, these combined easily enough with the fast-developing cinema (the 'talkies' came in during the decade), Henry Hall, the Brains Trust and the popular week-end papers. It was here that the James Douglases occasionally, and profitably, exposed the wickedness and profligacy of the two per cent by writing articles about them for the horrified enjoyment of the ninety-eight.

It was among only a fraction of this two per cent that the thinking of Sigmund Freud and Havelock Ellis was even then of much account. In the little world of those who write books and review each other's, where everyone is known to everyone, where

14

no two can gossip for five minutes without discovering a dozen mutual acquaintances (usually called 'great friends'), it was fashionable to accept – or invent – Freudian explanations for everything. It was a moral and philosophical climate that merits, for the purposes of this book, a brief digression on the subject of what Freud had done.

What Freud had done was to adopt an existing theory (started by Professor Charcot, the Parisian neurologist) about the 'psychic' origin of hysteria, and develop from it a theory that ideas can produce physical changes. He first tried cure by hypnosis, and then went on to suggestion, the significance of dreams, and the 'discovery' that nearly all cases of neurosis were due to the repression of sexual desires – which, he said, begin at birth and not at puberty. There is a 'natural man', a rather elemental and unattractive character, imprisoned within each one of us and usually but dangerously ignored. He possesses the power to identify himself with our decent and innocent thoughts, giving them demoniacal energy. To enable him to do this rationally and usefully is one of the main purposes of psycho-analysis; but because of the inner man, the unconscious mind, the 'id', and his association with repressed sexual desires, a new fear ran through the Fleet Street pubs in the late 'twenties.

Was sex going to become rational and even respectable? What would the popular 'Sundays' do, when they could no longer popularly condemn on their leader pages what they popularly wrote about, depicted and titillated on all the others? Trenchant condemnation of the new moral climate was called for. No one condemned more trenchantly than James Douglas, who had read not only about Freud but

15

about Havelock Ellis. And here was this Havelock Ellis actually declaring publicly – in a preface to it – that a book about lesbianism was a book about people 'of the highest character and the finest aptitudes' and that their 'relation to the often hostile society in which they move presents difficult and still unsolved problems'. Havelock Ellis, Mr Douglas noted with scorn, found in this awful book 'poignant situations set forth so vividly, and yet with such complete absence of offence, that we must place Radclyffe Hall's book on a high level of distinction'.

'Undiscussable', yelled Douglas, proceeding to discuss it in the good old Sunday morning way. 'Seductive and insidious special pleading designed to display perverted decadence as a martyrdom inflicted upon these outcasts by a cruel society ... literature as well as morality is in peril.' And then he hit upon the phrase by which, and by nothing else, he will be remembered, now that *The Well of Loneliness* has become a gentle, euphemistic and decorous plea for a tortured and potentially valuable section of humanity. 'I would rather,' he wrote, 'give a healthy boy or a healthy girl a phial of prussic acid than this novel. Poison kills the body, but moral poison kills the soul.'

There were other things to be afraid of, too. There was Dr Marie Stopes. She was actually and deliberately encouraging men and (worse) women to believe that sexual congress was something to be enjoyed for its own sake, rather than a home-taught manufacturing process with overtones of wicked excitement. If once this idea got firmly established, nothing could ever stop the working classes going in for it. The family would perish, marriage would disappear with it, and the only single respect in which we should be any different from the beasts of the field would be

16

that they didn't know why they were doing it and we did.

There was also John Baird. It was in that fateful year, 1928, that he achieved his first transatlantic television transmission – and also demonstrated colour television in this country. And it was only two years since he had shown a small audience at the Royal Institution that television was possible at all. Now there are many ways of exaggerating what television has done to and for us, but it is not possible to exaggerate its ease of access to the mass mind nor its capacity to create and spread ideas. James Douglas may not have been among the visionaries who saw what television was going to bring, but if he could know what it was disseminating today he would be revolving giddily in his grave. Radclyffe Hall's much-maligned book may not have been the literary or moral watershed that, in retrospect, it now sometimes seems to have been, but it helped to make 1928 an eventful year in the human saga of self-discovery.

Of course, in reading Havelock Ellis's opening 'commentary' on the book, and thinking of James Douglas's reaction to it, one is reduced to something like total despair about the value of language as a vehicle of communication between man and man.

*   *   *

Apart from the moral climate suggested by the success of the books and authors already mentioned, where did *The Well of Loneliness* stand in terms of literary merit? The 'established' popular novelists in the public libraries, and those who had attained the (now unattainable) dignity of standard editions, were such as Jeffery Farnol, William J. Locke, Ethel M.

17

Dell, Francis Brett Young and Warwick Deeping. They told good stories and told them in front of the children. Their novels were discreet and drew veils. The intimacies of life and those things that the ninety-eight per cent discussed only monastically and in swear-words, were represented by asterisks. Stoddard King versified their prototype:

'A writer owned an asterisk and kept it in
    his den
Where he wrote tales (which had large sales)
Of erring maids and men;
And always when he reached the point
    where carping censors lurk
He called upon the asterisk to do his dirty
    work.'

There was a style of the time, a prose blend, if you like, of George R. Sims, Rupert Brooke and Wilhelmina Stitch. A passage from *The Well of Loneliness* could have come from any of them:

'The strange, implacable heart – broken music of hounds giving tongue as they break from cover; the cry of the huntsman as he stands in his stirrups; the thud of hooves pounding ruthlessly forward over long, green undulating meadows. The meadows flying back as though seen from a train, the meadows streaming away behind you; the acrid smell of horse sweat caught in passing; the smell of damp leather, of earth and bruised herbage – all sudden, all passing – then the smell of wide spaces, the air smell, cool yet as potent as wine.'

18

Discuss derivation, as the contemporary English examiners might have said. And:

> 'Came the day when Mary refused to see Martin, when she turned upon Stephen, pale and accusing: "Can't you understand? Are you utterly blind – have you only got eyes now for Valerie Seymour?" And as though she were suddenly smitten dumb, Stephen's lips remained closed and she answered nothing.'

The threefold repetition in that last sentence vividly recalls the period – when paper was plentiful, blue pencils lay idle, writers drooled on and on, and tautology took the place of construction. James Douglas himself was one of its high priests – 'They were blind in their patience,' he wrote of the war's returning wounded soldiers, 'they were myopic in their forbearance.'

But – back to Miss Radclyffe Hall:

> 'They were long, these dinners, overloaded with courses; they were heavy, being weighted with polite conversation; they were stately, by reason of the family silver; above all they were firmly conservative in spirit, as conservative as the marriage service itself and almost as insistent upon sex distinction.'

Thus at least she would be keeping her eye on the central concern of her story and not *merely* word-spinning. It was all in the contemporary Came-the-Dawn tradition, but there are passages in *The Well of*

Loneliness that entitle the book to serious literary appraisal. *The Times Literary Supplement* called it 'sincere, courageous, high-minded and often beautifully expressed'. But it was *what* it expressed that they were being asked to think about in the 'twenties; and the denial of homosexuality, in particular the determined pretence that it could not exist among women, was so vital to them that even the *Annual Register*'s anonymous reviewer felt constrained to say:

> 'The book, despite its merits' (which he left unspecified) 'has too much the air of a personal crusade to compare favourably with its author's previous prize-winning book, *Adam's Breed.*'

To its modern reader (are there any?) it would probably have no such air if it were not for the now known personality of its author. It is not today, and it wasn't then, clinical or detached enough as propaganda. It was impassioned at a time when passionate writing seemed to belong half a century back with Dickens and Charles Reade.

And it was in 1920 that the House of Lords (which excluded women), debating a Sexual Offences Bill that in due course became the Criminal Law Amendment Act of 1922, tried to make lesbianism criminal. Only thirty-five years earlier the House of Commons had been rushed, indeed almost tricked, into enacting a penalty of two years' imprisonment for private sexual acts between men; and on that occasion the opportunity seized – by Henry Labouchère in an almost empty House after midnight – was also afforded by a Criminal Law Amendment Bill. In both cases the proposal was totally irrelevant to the declared purpose of the Bill itself; but in 1920 their Lordships had before them the knowledge that the Act of 1885* (with its 'Labouchère Amendment') had brought needless ruin upon a multitude of good citizens and wholly unmerited odium upon their families. The 1920 attempt to do the same for women failed ignominiously, but the prurient masculine self-righteousness that inspired it was soon to find a new champion in James Douglas.

*   *   *

Under the law as it stands today, as Mr Richard du Cann points out on another page, Miss Radclyffe Hall and her publisher would be better able to defend their book. But in one respect the law has changed not at all. Win or lose, the victim of such an attack will get no help about his costs.

Radclyffe Hall was a well-to-do woman in her own right. But she sold her house to pay the costs that the case involved her in. If in 1928 there had been any provision for 'legal aid' in such cases, she would have been well above any conceivable income limit laid down. The Poor Prisoners' Defence Act was not to come until two years later (crowning with success a long campaign by the Howard League for Penal Reform); but it too would have been useless to anyone like Radclyffe Hall, even if she had officially been a defendant. Today the Criminal Justice Act of 1967 greatly extends the scope of legal aid *in criminal*

---

* The reason why lesbians were not included in this Bill is attributed to Queen Victoria who, when asked for her assent, expressed complete ignorance of female inversion or perversion and therefore refused to sign the Bill, unless all reference to such practices was omitted.

cases; but, again, this would avail no one in her position, even as a penniless defendant, since legal aid for the needy in the Magistrates' Courts is available only for matrimonial and domestic disputes and criminal charges. Being 'required to show cause why a book should not be destroyed' comes within neither of these categories, for it is not 'a criminal cause or matter'. A small-time bookseller faced with this task and proposing to employ solicitor and counsel will therefore have to pay for them himself – win or lose.

And when in 1967 Sir Cyril Black, M.P., decided, as a private litigant, to show the police and the Attorney-General that *Last Exit to Brooklyn* was an irredeemably obscene book, financially he won but a Pyrrhic victory. When the Bow Street Magistrate, asked to award Sir Cyril all or some of his £1,000 costs, looked into the Statutes that might have enabled him to do so, he found, to his own surprise and Sir Cyril's consternation, that none of them did. There is no justice in this; and the complacency of Parliament and the lawyers about it is staggering. 'The Criminal Justice Act 1967,' said an article in *The New Law Journal* on 28th December 1967, 'contains very substantial reforms, but as there appears to be no evidence of any comparable concern about the law in regard to costs in criminal cases, it is to be assumed that Parliament is satisfied with the existing situation.' And the existing situation is chaotic, the chaos being concealed by the variety of empirical dodges to which the Magistrates' Clerks and the police have had compulsory recourse for more than a century.

You do not have to be in sympathy with Sir Cyril Black's campaign (I'm not) to see that the private citizen should not have to bear the cost of a prosecution which the Court's decision establishes as justly brought. Or if you are in doubt about this, it should be resolved when you are reminded that an *unsuccessful* private litigant in such a case can be ordered to pay all the costs of the bookseller, publisher and author and sent to prison if he fails or refuses. This was deliberately made possible by the Obscene Publications Act of 1959, as a solatium for the Government's refusal to have all cases conducted by the Director of Public Prosecutions. The law is therefore saying, to people like Sir Cyril Black, 'heads we win, tails you lose'. Weep not, perhaps, for Sir Cyril Black, who is not a poor man. Weep, if you like, for the publishers of *Last Exit to Brooklyn,* for whom the costs of this and the subsequent trial on indictment are said to have exceeded £30,000. But can we be proud of a system which still pronounces, as did Anatole France's *Crainquebille,* that 'the law, in its majestic equality, forbids the rich as well as the poor to sleep under bridges, to beg in the streets, and to steal bread'?

*   *   *

I suppose one of the penalties attaching to a ministerial career in British political life is that no one bothers to question the type-casting legends which, as a rule, the man's name accumulates. As for Home Secretaries, it's hard to recall one with an untarnished image, but probably the most ridiculed and reviled of all Home Secretaries in the present century was Sir William Joynson-Hicks (later Lord Brentford), described in Mr A. J. P. Taylor's contribution to *The Oxford English History* (Vol. 15) as 'The Preposterous Jix'. Preposterous because he 'saw a Communist under every bed', authorised the prosecution of twelve leading communists for inciting soldiers to mutiny, fervently and effectively opposed the 'revised Prayer Book' during the very months that saw the condemnation of *The Well of Loneliness*, and directed the famous Special Branch raid on the Moorgate premises of ARCOS, the Russian Trade Delegation in Great Britain. But in those days many more people were frightened of Communism than would admit to it now; and Joynson-Hicks's phobia, having served its turn, had to be supplanted in the collective public memory by something more patently ridiculous and execrable. *The Well of Loneliness* case was just right.

However it wasn't Joynson-Hicks who went into action against the book. It was two men whose motives were diametrically opposed – James Douglas, who read it and thought that no one else should be allowed to, and (of all men) Jonathan Cape, who had published it. It was Cape's action in sending a copy of it to the Home Secretary for 'clearance' that made its prosecution almost inevitable. But for that we should probably never have heard any more of it. Home Office witnesses have always told enquiring committees on this subject that they take no responsibility in such matters. They are not a Board of Censors. They will neither condemn nor approve. Long before 1946, when the Prosecution of Offences Regulations made it obligatory, they sent all dubious books coming to their notice (and the Home Office itself doesn't go looking for them) to the Director of Public Prosecutions for him to decide on.

If you wanted to publish a book which *you* thought dubious, you could be certain that the Home Office, should you ask them, would think it dubious too. You might as well send it direct to the Director of Public

Prosecutions and ask *him,* thus saving the two or three months that it would take to get from Whitehall to Buckingham Gate. Sometimes, if you are sufficiently sophisticated, you can get an unofficial 'clearance' from the Attorney-General, as Weidenfeld & Nicolson did when they wanted to publish *Lolita.* But to send a 'dubious' book to the Home Office for approval, at least in the 'twenties, was like submitting the plans for a train robbery. 'The Preposterous Jix' was a man of his time as well as Home Secretary; and he was a lawyer as well as being a leading Evangelical, who wrote books on the censorship of morals. It was Miss Radclyffe Hall's just complaint that her book was sent to the Home Office without any attempt to ascertain her own wishes. She was a wealthy woman. If her author's contract did not already hold the publisher blameless (as it would today), she might well have urged publication *pace* James Douglas and indemnified Cape's against possible loss.

*   *   *

I can think of no more poignant illustration of the Pecksniffian 1928 attitude to sexual inversion than what the *New Statesman* (alas) wrote in a leader on the 24th November, 1928:

> 'The authoress, it seems to us, made two mistakes: first, in writing the book at all – for people who desire tolerance for pathological abnormalities certainly should not write about them – and, second, in deliberately inviting the judgment of the Home Office upon her work.'*

* The full text of this leader can be found on page 115.

25

Can you imagine the *New Statesman,* of all papers, writing detachedly of 'people who desire tolerance' (as distinct, presumably, from punishment and execration) 'for pathological abnormalities'? Would this be the paper, even so, that advocated silent suffering rather than any impassioned plea for new thinking and a new morality? One can forgive its having been misled about who sent the book to the Home Office; and Radclyffe Hall's solicitors wrote promptly to put the record straight. But in 1928 the problem of inversion was not new, or newly being ventilated, in the circles where the *New Statesman* was read. It was even understood to be something utterly different from the problem of perversion – which, whether it is reprehensible or not, is at least deliberate and self-sought. There is still a thought barrier to be broken through before 'inverts' can have any part in shared human happiness; 'few societies,' as Dr Edmund Leach said in his uncomfortable and comfortless Reith Lectures in 1967, 'have ever been so ruthlessly intolerant of abnormality as is our own'; but in 1928 it seems not to have been realised that the barrier even existed. You cannot attack or surmount any difficulty until you know it is there.

In *Man and Society,* the journal of the Albany Trust, a professional woman wrote about 'Loneliness' in August 1963. She wrote of 'the evil which comes from a wholly negative attitude, a philosophy that the avoidance of deviations in conduct is worth any price in terms of the strangulation of sincere feeling ...' She went on: 'Nothing but someone to love can make the prospect of old age and death tolerable or rescue one from the encrustations of selfishness. But by now my feelings have been so well conditioned by our restrictive culture that I probably could no longer love any woman . . . I am a triumph of conventional morality, a tribute to its power to enforce the burial of "that one talent which 'tis death to hide". Against all advice I refuse to insure for my old age because I do not intend to have an old age if it is to be solitary. Solitude gradually destroys one's intelligence, will-power, self-respect, personality, everything,' she concluded, and it is true of a great number of people, though not of all. 'It seems obvious that a deeper morality would require first of all the recognition that *a relationship of love between any two people is in itself a better thing than a relationship of indifference or hate.*'

The italics are mine. They epitomise what Radclyffe Hall set out to say in her big, rambling, over-written and desperately sincere book.

Exactly forty years after the ludicrous uproar about *The Well of Loneliness,* toleration and compassion can perhaps be seen to have made some advance. This book, anyway, will not be sent to the Home Secretary and no police officer will say in Court that he finds it shocking. (In 1964 Parliament withdrew legal recognition from any such policemanly susceptibilities: the Obscene Publications Act of that year amended the 1959 statute, which had run into difficulties about the non-corruptibility of policemen, so that 'publication' of a book to some corruptible person was no longer necessary. It became an offence merely to 'have it for publication for gain'.)

Women like those for whom Radclyffe Hall was speaking are known among us all as good citizens, good neighbours, often – at immense cost to themselves in nervous energy and worry – good mothers. In relation to homosexuality in men, the Sexual Offences Act of 1967 has recognised at last the abysmal

27

stupidity of official punishment as an expression of society's distaste, retaining only the sanctions necessary to protect minors and public order. In relation to both men and women, the ancestral stupidity will not, for many years to come, be greatly influenced by what the law may say. There are multitudes of men and women, there are priests, and there are even doctors, who do not know the difference between perversion and inversion and who, if they did, would go on punishing the former and pretending that the latter did not exist.

I suppose one sign of advance is that the sex joke is losing value in the currency of virile conversation and belongs to the fatuous vocabulary of the 'I say, I say, I say' school of comedians, dead these many years but with nowhere to lie down. Sex has become rather more serious than funny. 'The time will come,' as W. N. P. Barbellion said, 'when a joke about sex will be not so much objectionable as unintelligible. To the perfectly enfranchised mind it should be as impossible to joke about sex as about mind or digestion or physiology.' We are still joking about all four, but the work of Radclyffe Hall brought perceptibly nearer the day of the 'perfectly enfranchised mind'.

Bramley, Surrey, 1968   C. H. Rolph

1

THE LIFE STORY OF RADCLYFFE HALL
UP TO *THE WELL OF LONELINESS*

IN SPITE of all the tendentious attacks on her which followed the publication of *The Well of Loneliness,* Radclyffe Hall remains one of the least publicised of well-known authors.

The only biography of her, by Una Troubridge, appeared in the Spring of 1945 soon after her death. It is a short book, in the form of a long letter, written between February 19th and March 18th of that year, which covers less than two hundred small printed pages.

The facts collected in Una's artless narrative are sporadic, and make little attempt at logical arrangement. Its chief value lies in the evidence that it provides of selfless, uncalculating affection, of a kind that seldom exists between individuals of either sex. Needless to say it has no index, but supplies some useful photographs, mostly unobtainable elsewhere. Una Troubridge herself died in November, 1963, leaving only one daughter. This daughter was killed in a motor accident in 1966, and such papers as the mother and daughter left are now in Canada.

Her book tells us something, but not much, about Radclyffe Hall, who must have been one of the least educated writers to achieve representation in the National Portrait Gallery. How was it, the reader inevitably asks, that this gifted woman, who achieved an outstanding *succès d'estime* with her third publication, came so late to literary renown?

The answer lies partly in an upbringing and circumstances unusual for a writer. She was a well-to-do young girl who inherited a substantial income from a handsome, irresponsible father, Radclyffe Radclyffe-Hall, the only son of Dr Charles Radclyffe-Hall, an eminent physician who specialised in treating tuberculosis. The dissolute young man, a chronic victim of asthma, became her mother's second husband, and was divorced by her when their daughter was three.

This daughter, who closely resembled her good-looking father both in her blue eyes and fair hair, and her life-long affection for dogs, was never taught to work, and work seems to have been the last accomplishment that anyone expected of her. She lived with her mother and maternal grandmother and was inappropriately christened 'Marguerite' – a name soon dropped in favour of 'Peter' and then, more permanently, of 'John'. Her father, who periodically visited her and became interested in her when her

30

good looks developed, died from pulmonary trouble when she was eighteen. Belatedly conscious of his responsibilities, he enquired on his last visit about her studies and aims in life, and urged her to keep to one pursuit and not to be 'a Jack of all trades as I have been'.

Her 'education' had consisted only of occasional attendance at day-schools, and a year at King's College, London. Until the age of thirty-four she was, in the frank words of Una Troubridge, 'bone idle', living on her wealth and doing whatever she fancied. Like her father, who had some slight talent for music and painting and, according to Una, 'scrambled through Eton and Oxford', she had no natural capacity for application and industry. These, largely self-generated, came later when she had discovered her considerable gift for writing, and developed the impulse to use it.

An uncomfortable family life had left the young woman with little enthusiasm for home ties. Her mother, Mary Jane Diehl of Philadelphia, was American, and had married for the first time in America. Radclyffe owed nothing whatever to this brainless and egotistical mother, who had lost her first daughter, and so little wanted her second that she tried every possible expedient to prevent her birth. Eventually Mrs Radclyffe-Hall married, as her third husband, her Italian teacher of singing, Alberto Visetti, capable enough in his profession, but useless even as a pseudo-parent. Una Troubridge records his decision, when his step-daughter was eleven, to give away her much loved pet canary to a waiter at a Belgian hotel, on the ground that the bird and its cage had become an 'encumbrance'.

Radclyffe, who early developed a dominant instinct

to protect any creature which was young and weak, suffered hours of misery speculating on the fate of her beloved canary in the hands of strangers. The only real affection she knew in childhood came from her kindly but incompetent grandmother, so much bullied by her own disagreeable daughter that, as soon as escape became legally possible on her twenty-first birthday, young Radclyffe Hall took her away to a house in Kensington which they shared for several years.

Until then, she lived with her mother and step-father in a large house in Earl's Court, where Signor Visetti, now Professor of Singing attached to the Royal College of Music, successfully followed his profession. Her mother, who quarrelled with her husband incessantly, made no secret of her dislike for her daughter ('Your hands,' she would say peevishly, 'are just like Radclyffe's') but did not hesitate to use the daughter's fortune from the Radclyffe-Hall Trust to promote her own social aspirations. The only advantage that came to Radclyffe from these domestic arrangements was their musical background, for at quite an early age she showed outstanding musical capacity and a talent for improvisation and composi-tion, though the necessary discipline for the develop-ment of these gifts was always lacking.

During her adolescence her stepfather's guests included Nikisch, the great German conductor. He listened to her performance on the piano and was so much impressed by her original talent that he asked her to put everything else on one side and come to Germany to study composition as his pupil, even though he discovered that she could not read a note of music and did not know in what key she was playing. But she was not then ready for the discipline of hard

Radclyffe Hall at the age of five. Oil painting by Katinka Amyat

Radclyffe Hall in 1918. Oil painting by Charles Buchel

work, though she had composed verses from her earliest childhood, and soon began to compose at the piano, fitting the words to her own settings so that poems and music came to fruition together.

The words were written down and many of the poems subsequently published, including one entitled 'The Last Cuckoo', which was accepted by Chappel & Company and sung by several well-known singers. But the settings remained only in her memory, and as she was incapable of transcribing them were usually forgotten. The desultory character of this work and its unsatisfactory transience may well have been a factor in her subsequent conversion to the painful perseverance which marked her writings.

She was very good-looking and, in spite of her educational shortcomings, was full of charm and intelligence. She systematically over-smoked, including green cigars, and had a strong head, but never drank to excess, for nicotine was her craving.

From the age of seventeen, she fell periodically in and out of love with members of her own sex. A suspicion that Radclyffe was not 'normal' may have lain at the root of her mother's dislike, though she had been a beautiful child. A portrait painted at the age of five by Mrs Katinka Amyat, the leading child portrait painter of her day, shows a substantial-looking toddler with large blue eyes, short fair hair, and sturdy unfeminine arms, who could equally well have been a boy or a girl. She is most unsuitably dressed in a frilly smock which recalls the voluminous muslins worn by the actress Wilette Kershaw, who played the part of Stephen Gordon in the drama-tised Paris version of *The Well of Loneliness*.

An oil painting by Charles Buchel of the adult Radclyffe Hall made soon after she met Una

Troubridge – then a pretty but insipid-looking girl with a short nose and blonde hair, smoothly combed back from her forehead, who was only in her twenties and about ten years younger than Radclyffe Hall – shows her wearing a loose-fitting coat and shirt with a high collar. Being well-made and well-proportioned, she appeared taller than she really was. Later she cut off her hair, which she wore twisted tightly round her small head, though short hair in adult women was then thought rather shocking. She always disliked showy, decorative clothes, and once lay flat on her face in Kensington Gardens in a new white plush coat as a protest against being displayed in her mailcart wearing this extravagant feminine garment.

Other indications of her complex personality emerged in a dislike of dolls and a fondness for noisy toys such as drums. Her poem *Salvation,* quoted on the flyleaf of Una Troubridge's book *The Life and Death of Radclyffe Hall,* conforms to this tendency:

'I will be bold and unafraid,
And great with high endeavour,
And all the trumpets men have made
And all the drums that men have played,
They shall be mine for ever.
There'll be a noise, a mighty noise,
Of bugling and drumming
When I go out to Jericho,
Across the plains to Jericho,
In the good time that's coming!'

Assuming that she was not thinking in terms of the hereafter, this optimistic forecast of her own future proved to be quite unjustified, for she died of inoperable cancer at the relatively early age of sixty after an experience of humiliation and painful abuse which seldom assails a woman of her social status. Both the abuse and the terrible illness were borne with great fortitude, which she had never lacked; it was perhaps the keynote of her character.

One friend who met both Radclyffe Hall and Una Troubridge at the time that *The Well of Loneliness* was published, describes them as they appeared when visiting tea-rooms in the Buckingham Palace Road.

'My first impression was of someone very good-looking, in fact handsome, in a masculine way. She was dressed in tweedy style, mannishly cut clothes. She had a presence and an air of authority. Later on I saw her often in the Tea Rooms with Lady Troubridge, who was also one of my father's customers. Lady Troubridge was the exact opposite – very dainty and feminine and like Radclyffe Hall was very well dressed, but in an opposite way. Radclyffe Hall's clothes were mannish to the nth degree – Lady Troubridge was exquisitely, femininely dressed in a rather "fluffy" style. My mother used to say that Radclyffe Hall always seemed to be the dominant one in any decision which had to be made jointly, regarding their orders for refreshments, cakes to be made and sent, and their Christmas orders for chocolates.'

One member of the Society of Women Writers and Journalists, Kathleen Lee, recalls working for the *Sunday Times* in 1927, when she was invited to meet Radclyffe Hall on an occasion when several impressive guests were present.

'I had already admired her works,' wrote Miss Lee, 'and my admiration was extended to her because of her kind words and friendly manner. She was wearing

35

a smart plain hat and dark suit and I particularly noticed the large rings on her forefinger and thumb, dull silver with big single stones, not sparkling, so they must have been semi-precious. Later on in the cloakroom I heard someone ask Miss Hall the title of her new book, and then say, "No, better not tell. Supposed to bring bad luck".'

She adds: 'When *The Well of Loneliness* was published, a senior mistress on the staff of the school where I was only a middling had said we all ought to read it before it was banned, as the papers were hinting it would be. In my turn I had the loan and sat up nearly all night reading it. The storm astonished me. I just thought it a very fine story and did not understand what the fuss was all about. I realise now that I was very naïve but I am still of the same opinion.

'Losing no time I rushed off a letter to *John O'London's,* commending the book and denouncing Government folly. Needless to say it was printed! I had a very kind note of thanks from Radclyffe Hall which I kept for years.'

Radclyffe Hall's clear-cut features, characteristic of neither a man nor a woman and yet of both, were peculiarly memorable. Even after forty years I recall with extreme clarity the red, congested face of the elderly magistrate Sir Chartres Biron, to whom Radclyffe Hall represented the limit of conscious depravity, and the pale, intense face of the woman whose contours suggested those of a handsome man in early middle age courting martyrdom, with a determined identification of herself with the misunderstood minority, which she regarded as her mission in life to explain and defend.

Before these years her affairs with other women

had been incessant. She herself has told us that she first fell in love with a woman's voice – the pure beautiful soprano of the singer Agnes Nichols, a pupil of her stepfather. Una Troubridge assures us that, but for the accident of illness, Agnes Nichols, seven years the senior of Radclyffe Hall, would have sung the solo at her Requiem Mass in 1943.

Other romances, before Radclyffe Hall's overall love story with Una Troubridge, included a long and emotional relationship with Mabel Veronica Batten (Mrs George Batten), Una's cousin, and twenty-four years the senior of Radclyffe Hall. This relationship began when Radclyffe Hall was twenty-seven, and continued up to the death of Mrs Batten early in the First World War. It changed the whole course of Radclyffe's existence and transformed her outlook on life.

When they first met in Hamburg, Mrs Batten was a beautiful woman of fifty, with a pale complexion, dark blue eyes and dark hair, and a perfectly shaped tip-tilted nose. She was not only lovely, but keenly intelligent and highly cultured. Her husband, once Secretary to the Viceroy of India, was twenty-five years her senior and treated her with the indulgence of a devoted father.

As an acknowledged patroness of music, she had sponsored the pianist Percy Grainger and the young Mischa Elman, and was herself a relatively talented composer. She read assiduously in French as well as English, and had some knowledge of Italian. She accepted homage as her right and appreciated admiration, but had no intention of conferring her affection upon a young barbarian who preferred hunting and dogs to music and literature.

Radclyffe's unconcealed adoration moved 'Ladye',

37

as her friends all called her, to the uncompromising comment that people who had loved and been loved by her had always used their brains, and had generally been persons of significance. This challenge was not lost on the future author, whose real education began with her endeavour to meet it. Shortly after the beginning of their acquaintance, Radclyffe was thrown when riding by a bad-tempered jumper known as Xenophon, who crashed into a ditch when an ill-mannered amateur crossed him and brought him down at a fence. Radclyffe insisted on riding the ten miles home, but she suffered severely from shock and concussion and for weeks was seriously ill. As she was a very good sailor and, like her father loved the sea, her doctors suggested a sea voyage. The upshot was that she and Mrs Batten left England together, on a journey to the Canaries.

This arrangement not only furthered her education but caused a rapid decline in her sporting pre-occupations, in spite of her affection for the horses that she kept and the dogs she continued to breed. By the end of their holiday together the love-affair between herself and Mabel Batten, which continued to the end of Ladye's life, had reached a point when neither could abandon it. Ladye, who disliked English country life, especially in the winter, was neither 'horsey' nor 'doggy'; in fact she feared horses and had no use for them, while she was accustomed to holidays in Morocco, Corsica, Rome and Monte Carlo.

These divergent ways of life could not be combined, and as Ladye was the senior and dominant partner, her tastes prevailed. Radclyffe herself was now beginning to see brain as more important than muscle and, by the time she came to know Una Troubridge in 1915, she had not ridden a horse for years. She had also developed humanitarian instincts, already associated with her horror of stag-hunting, and Ladye's way of life suited her better than the pursuits of the unregenerate past. If they had not met, neither *The Well of Loneliness* nor Radclyffe's seven other novels might ever have been written. Ladye was delighted by the dawning of a talent which she was well able to recognise, and soon began to take steps which led, indirectly and long after her death, to the creation of the books by which Radclyffe Hall is known.

At that time her intimate friendship with Una Troubridge lay in the future, though her love relationship with Ladye was terminated by her death in 1916. During that winter and early spring, as Ladye's health was indifferent and she felt disinclined for a wartime journey into the country, Radclyffe and Una, who was then living in London in a small house in Bryanston Square, travelled together to Malvern where Radclyffe owned a house known as White Cottage which she had decided to sell. She and Ladye had bought it together and dearly loved it, but the rising prices of war-time compelled its disposal. Many of the West Country scenes so vividly depicted in *The Well of Loneliness* owe their inspiration to her ownership of this cottage.

The tragedy that altered the direction of Radclyffe's life came with shocking suddenness. On May 10th she and Una had arranged to spend a day at Maidenhead inspecting a bulldog puppy. They left Ladye preparing to sing at an afternoon party. When Una returned rather later than she had intended to her London flat, she received a telephone call from Ladye asking if Radclyffe was on her way home. This was the case. An hour later 'John' herself rang up to ask for the name of Una's doctor, since their own was

39

not available. Ladye, she said, had become suddenly ill and was complaining of pins and needles all down one side. This was the beginning of a gradual but conclusive cerebral haemorrhage. By the time Una reached Radclyffe's hotel, Ladye's power of speech was gone and, though she lingered for another fortnight, she never spoke lucidly again.

The stroke was subsequently thought to have originated in a serious accident to Ladye's car on the way to White Cottage, in which Radclyffe, who was with her, had been unhurt, but Ladye was seriously injured and remained an invalid, suffering from high blood pressure for several months.

Radclyffe now reproached herself bitterly for leaving Ladye for the day's visit to Maidenhead, and turned to Una for consolation – which remained unfailing to the end of Radclyffe's life. Too numbed with grief to feel any personal concern for Una at first, she conceived an affection which was steadily to develop and became in the end essential to them both. Finally they established a joint home at Cadogan Court, remained together throughout the First World War, and were never parted again for more than a few days at a time, during the twenty-seven years that remained of Radclyffe's life.

Radclyffe's other friends, both earlier and later, inevitably also became Una's. Among them was the novelist and film producer, R. J. Minney, who between the years 1925 and 1942 was also Editor of *Everybody's Weekly,* the *Sunday Referee* and later the *Strand Magazine* which he left to go into films. As most of Radclyffe Hall's correspondence has disappeared, a letter from her to Mr Minney in 1935 has some rarity value. It is quoted here for this reason and also because it casts some light on her methods of working. The letter, written in manuscript on both sides of a sheet of yellow notepaper, runs as follows:

'Beauvallon. Var.
France.
23.5.35.

'Dear R. J. Minney,

'I am getting Una Troubridge to write this letter as I must save my hand because having no typist out here I am not only (as I always do) writing my new book, but I am doing all the polishing and recopying which I usually dictate. I want to explain my apparent rudeness in never writing to you after you sent me the proofs of your novel to read.

'The fact is that just at that time Una Troubridge became very unwell and it was discovered that there was some heart trouble probably resulting from a lung operation she had three years ago, and I was so desperately worried that books and everything else went out of my mind. Indeed it is only now when she is really getting some benefit out here, where I was told to bring her, that I have been able to stop worrying and get down to my new book which I began last month.

'Will you please understand and forgive my negligence? I never read anything while I am on my own book so shall have to leave yours until mine goes to the publishers. Edgar Wallace is my highest flight when I am writing myself.

'I expect to be here 3 months and then in

England for a while, but *not* in St. Martin's Lane which we had to part with as the doctors said Una T. must not do stairs. You must come down and lunch with us in Rye when we return; she joins me in kind regards.

Yours v. sincerely,
Radclyffe Hall.'

Other friends included such well-known personalities as Edith Craig, Christopher St John, Tony Atwood, Francis Yeats-Brown, and Naomi Jacob at Sirmione on Lake Garda. It is justifiable to assume that some of these men and women had homosexual interests or tendencies. There is no doubt that one was Naomi Jacob, who made no secret of the fact. Her style of dressing was far more aggressively masculine than that of Radclyffe Hall; she wore dress suits in the evening, and few men had a greater addiction to the whisky bottle.

Naomi Jacob came late into Radclyffe Hall's life, but their friendship, which began with the publication of *The Well of Loneliness,* developed very rapidly. Naomi bought it at the Times Bookshop on the day of publication, and 'found its sincerity very touching and fine'.

'Reading it in 1928,' Naomi Jacob wrote in *Me and the Swans* (1963), 'it would never have occurred to me that there was a single sentence or phrase which could be criticised on the ground of being immoral or offensive.'

In the idiom of that day, Radclyffe Hall was a 'lady', and her treatment of her delicate theme was essentially lady-like. Yet Naomi Jacob, vulgar and volatile as a street-urchin, touched a chord which brought an unexpected response. When she and Una wanted to stay in Sirmione where Naomi Jacob lived, they finally established themselves at the Albergo Catullo, and visited Naomi's villa every morning. The friendship, cemented by the affection of all three for Naomi's beloved Peke, Samminino, lasted even though Naomi was not always a soothing or even a tactful companion.

She insisted on her right to see Radclyffe Hall when 'John' was dying and was deservedly repudiated by Una Troubridge. Her portrait in *Me and the Swans* provided many details of 'John' which Una Troubridge does not give, though she records that neither Radclyffe Hall nor Una ever learned to use a typewriter. 'John' worked slowly, writing in clear legible handwriting on thick pale blue paper, which she acquired by permission of the writer, Colette, who used nothing else.

On one occasion, while staying at Southend, Naomi and Una saw the advertisement for a lecture by Radclyffe Hall. They obtained tickets with difficulty, as the hall was sold out. When they attended it, Naomi, an excellent and racy speaker herself, was not impressed by 'John's' attainments as a lecturer. Though she had a clear, pleasant voice, she tried, like so many intellectuals, to cram too many facts into a talk on *The Well of Loneliness,* and caused even that topic to lack fire and animation.

Naomi visited 'John' for the last time when she was in the London Clinic to see a specialist, shortly before her death. 'John's' bravery was astonishing, according to the specialist.

'But isn't she afraid? People are always afraid of cancer. She doesn't seem to have any fear at all.'

Naomi, deeply distressed and naturally emotional,

43

stumbled out of the Clinic blinded with tears, but she shared 'John's' faith in the goodness and wisdom of God. Radclyffe Hall, a deeply religious woman, believed implicitly in the Catholic faith, which she loved, and never regarded death as the end.

Their correspondence must have been considerable and would have added greatly to our scanty knowledge of 'John', but unfortunately these letters were destroyed during the Second World War.

Naomi quitted Sirmione, where she was living at this period, but all her papers were left in the care of Elsa, a confidential maid. As the Germans moved into Italy, Elsa destroyed all Naomi's documents, including her letters from Radclyffe Hall, Alice Holtby and many others, as she feared that they might contain anti-Hitler material.

'Naomi always lamented about this,' a correspondent reported to me. 'The Germans painted red signs over the graves of her departed dogs.'

After the death of Mabel Batten, Radclyffe Hall was fortunate in finding a friend and lover whose devotion was so unqualified as that of Una Troubridge. In her biography of Radclyffe, Una mentions the books she read to 'John', especially those about the Brownings, whom they both loved and whose home had been near theirs in Florence. She describes one occasion on which she read aloud for eight hours on end, until her voice gave out under the strain.

'Thy love for me was wonderful,' runs David's famous lament for Jonathan in the Second Book of the Kings. 'I am distressed for thee, my brother Jonathan, very pleasant hast thou been unto me; thy love for me was wonderful, passing the love of women.'

This passage suggests a special quality in the love

44

of women for men, as distinct from the love of men for men. Apart from Ruth and Naomi, those respect-worthy symbols of orthodox friendship, there is little in the Scriptures, or indeed in all literature, to suggest the intensity of love which can exist between woman and woman. But Una Troubridge, for all her sim-plicity, indicates that it may very occasionally have a quality with which the romance of heterosexual rela-tionships cannot compete. Such love can exist between mother and daughter, sister and sister, or friend and friend; its distinction lies in its intensity, and its freedom from selfishness or the desire to possess. There is value in the very artlessness of Una Troubridge's narrative, which makes no attempt to disguise the undivided sincerity of her emotion.

Her biography of Radclyffe Hall, in addition to describing their friends, tells of their numerous houses, furnished and unfurnished, both at home and abroad; their pets, from ungainly horses to a tiny self-centred black-faced griffon called Ratou; their journeys overseas; Radclyffe Hall's publishing vicis-situdes; and the wearisome 'trolley' books, never intended to be more than time-filling exercises be-tween one serious work and another. A more experi-enced writer would probably not have needed to waste her time on them at all.

Una also records the last moments of Radclyffe Hall the day before she died, when in the throes of suffering she looked up at the nurse with the ghost of her jaunty smile and exclaimed: 'What a life!' Then quickly, and characteristically, adding: 'But I offer it to God.'

Two lines in Una's last letter from Radclyffe Hall, who always believed that her friend would survive her are characteristic: 'God keep you until we meet again

... and believe in my love, which is much, much stronger than mere death ...'

But never from beginning to end does the book explain precisely how and why these women were inverts, or the significance of inversion as a problem. For this we have to turn to *The Well of Loneliness* itself, with its uninhibited descriptions of frustration and pain.

Yet without some investigation of the problem in its various aspects, the actual hearing of the case seems to lack point as an important social phenomenon.

2

THE PROBLEM OF INVERSION

AMONG THE review books sent to me, an eager and relatively juvenile free-lance journalist, by *Time and Tide* in August 1928, was a novel which offered far more of a challenge to intelligence and toleration than the average publication which reaches an Editor's desk. *The Well of Loneliness* faced any viewer with a difficult problem; social, moral and literary. It was not a challenge which could be ignored. Confronting it as squarely as I could, I wrote my review under the somewhat obvious title 'Facing Facts'.

* * *

47

'In the first two of the books here reviewed, the authors are determined to face certain of the facts of life, though they may torture their minds and rend their hearts in so doing. The third novel makes a similar but less successful endeavour, since an altogether disproportionate significance is attached to the facts faced. The fourth story, which lays no claim to the painful art of realism, has nothing whatever in common with the others.

'Miss Radclyffe Hall's important, sincere and very moving study demands consideration from two different standpoints. In the first place, it is presented as a novel, and is therefore open to criticism as a work of imagination, a creative effort which challenges comparison with other examples of fiction. In the second place it is a plea, passionate, yet admirably restrained and never offensive, for the extension of social toleration, compassion and recognition to the biologically abnormal woman, who, because she possesses the tastes and instincts of a man, is too often undeservedly treated as a moral pariah.

'Many critics maintain that propaganda, of whatever kind, impairs a work of art. True as this aesthetic canon may be for the majority of such works, the fact remains that it is the problem which it discusses, rather than its rank in fiction, which lends to Miss Hall's book its undoubted significance. As a novel, written in language which is unfalteringly clear, sometimes beautiful and

48

often irritatingly Biblical, it is unduly long and overburdened with detail frequently irrelevant to the story's progress. Its shape is indefinite, and it leaves behind a sense of lost links which might have fastened its various parts more connectedly together, though in spite of these shortcomings it never fails to hold the absorbed attention of the reader. I believe, however, that it was by her theme, rather than by the form in which that theme was embodied, that the author intended her book to stand or fall; hence it is by her success or failure in dealing with the problem she has selected for treatment, that this particular example of her work must be judged.

'It may be said at once that *The Well of Loneliness* can only strengthen the belief of all honest and courageous persons that there is no problem which is not better frankly stated than concealed. Persecution and disgusted ostracism have never solved any difficulty in the world, and they certainly do not make the position of the female invert less bitter to herself or less dangerous to others. Miss Hall's dignified challenge, presenting without sentimentality or compunction the dreadful poignancy of ineradicable emotions, in comparison with which the emotions of normal men and women seem so clear and uncomplicated, certainly convinces us that women of the type of Stephen Gordon, in so far as their abnormality is inherent and not merely the unnecessary cult of exotic erotics, deserve the fullest consideration and compassion from all who are fortunate enough to have escaped one of Nature's cruellest dispensations.

'The book, however, raises and never satisfactorily answers another question – the question as to how far the characteristics of Stephen Gordon are physiological and how far they are psychological. Probably only an expert biologist could satisfactorily resolve such a difficulty. It certainly seems likely that a problem of this type must be intensified by the exaggeration of sex differences which has been peculiarly marked in certain ages of the world, and to which the English middle classes of the eighteenth and nineteenth centuries were particularly prone. Miss Hall appears to take for granted that this over-emphasis of sex characteristics is part of the correct education of the normal human being; she therefore makes her "normal" woman clinging and "feminine" to exasperation and even describes the attitudes towards love as "an end in itself" as being a necessary attribute to true womanhood. Many readers will know too many happy wives and mothers for whom it is not, to take on trust Miss Hall's selection of the qualities essential to one sex or the other.

'This confusion between what is "male" or "female" and what is merely human in our complex make-up, persists throughout the book. We feel that, in describing the supposedly sinister predilections of the child

Stephen Gordon, much ado is often made about nothing; so many of them appear to be the quite usual preferences of any vigorous young female who happens to possess more vitality and intelligence than her fellows. If one of the results of women's education in the eighteen-nineties really was to attach the ugly label "pervert" to a human being whose chief desire was for a wider expression of her humanity than contemporary convention permitted, then that education was an evil thing indeed. This is not to deny that the problem described by Miss Hall does exist in a grave and urgent form, and that her presentation of it deserves the serious attention of all students of social questions.'

'Ideologically,' wrote Alec Craig in 1937, 'the book adopts a very fair-minded point of view about a matter that causes a vast amount of human misery, and misery which is only exasperated by driving it underground. It faces, quite squarely and responsibly, the social difficulties which arise from the phenomena of which it treats. So far as normal people are concerned it could only act as a warning against relationships which are too often embarked upon in ignorance of their real nature. With regard to the invert, its only effect could be to bring a problem of human unhappiness out into the light of reason and knowledge instead of leaving it to breed additional and avoidable tragedy in the darkness of ignorance and superstition.'

On August 19th, exactly a week after my review appeared, came the famous broadside against *The*

Well of Loneliness by James Douglas, the sixty-year-old editor of the *Sunday Express*. It followed a review of the book by Robert Lynd in the *Daily News*. Magnificently established in his editorial chair on the side of the legions of righteousness, James Douglas advised his readers to insist that Radclyffe Hall's work should be suppressed. The photograph that accompanied his article showed a monstrous-looking figure with short hair and a bow tie. The heavy jaw (not characteristic of Radclyffe Hall), one hand in her pocket and a lighted cigarette in the other, were all calculated to be prejudicial to the readers of that day, in a fashion that a clever popular editor knows well how to achieve. In his article he wrote:

'*The Well of Loneliness* (Jonathan Cape, 15s. net) by Miss Radclyffe Hall, is a novel. The publishers state that it "handles very skilfully a psychological problem which needs to be understood in view of its growing importance.

' "In England hitherto," they admit, "the subject has not been treated frankly outside the regions of scientific text-books, but that its social consequences qualify a broader and more general treatment is likely to be the opinion of thoughtful and cultured people."

'They declare that they "have been deeply impressed by this study"; they have felt that such a book should not be lost to those who may be willing and able to understand and appreciate it. They believe that the author has treated the subject in such a way as to combine perfect frankness and sincerity with delicacy and deep psychological insight.

'In his prefatory "Commentary", Mr Havelock Ellis says: "I have read *The Well of Loneliness* with great interest because – apart from its fine qualities as a novel – it possesses a notable psychological and sociological significance.

' "So far as I know, it is the first English novel which presents, in a completely faithful and uncompromising form, one particular aspect of sexual life as it exists among us to-day.

' "The relation of certain people – who, while different from their fellow human beings, are sometimes of the highest character and the finest aptitudes – to the often hostile society in which they move presents difficult and still unsolved problems.

' "The poignant situations which thus arise are here set forth so vividly, and yet with such complete absence of offence, that we must place Radclyffe Hall's book on a high level of distinction."

'That is the defence and justification of what I regard as an intolerable outrage – the first outrage of the kind in the annals of English fiction.

'The defence is wholly unconvincing. The justification absolutely fails.

'In order to prevent the contamination and corruption of English fiction it is the duty of the critic to make it impossible for

53

any other novelist to repeat this outrage. I say deliberately that this novel is not fit to be sold by any bookseller or to be borrowed from any library.

'BRAVADO

'Its theme is utterly inadmissible in the novel, because the novel is read by people of all ages, by young women and young men as well as by older women and older men. Therefore, many things that are discussed in scientific text-books cannot decently be discussed in a work of fiction offered to the general reader.

'I am well aware that sexual inversion and perversion are horrors which exist among us today. They flaunt themselves in public places with increasing effrontery and more insolently provocative bravado. The decadent apostles of the most hideous and most loathsome vices no longer conceal their degeneracy and their degradation.

'They seem to imagine that there is no limit to the patience of the English people. They appear to revel in their defiance of public opinion. They do not shun publicity. On the contrary, they seek it, and they take a delight in their flamboyant notoriety. The consequence is that this pestilence is devastating the younger generation. It is wrecking young lives. It is defiling young souls.

'THE PLAGUE

'I have seen the plague stalking shamelessly through great social assemblies. I have

54

heard it whispered about by young men and young women who do not and cannot grasp its unutterable putrefaction. Both aspects of it are thrust upon healthy and innocent minds. The contagion cannot be escaped. It pervades our social life.

'Perhaps it is a blessing in disguise or a curse in disguise that this novel forces upon our society a disagreeable task which it has hitherto shirked, the task of cleaning itself from the leprosy of these lepers, and making the air clean and wholesome once more.

'I agree with Mr Havelock Ellis that this novel is "uncompromising". That is why criticism cannot compromise with it. The challenge is direct. It must be taken up courageously, and the fight must be fought to the finish. If our bookshops and our libraries are to be polluted by fiction dealing with this undiscussable subject, at least let us know where we are going.

'I know that the battle has been lost in France and Germany, but it has not yet been lost in England, and I do not believe that it will be lost. The English people are slow to rise in their wrath and strike down the armies of evil, but when they are aroused they show no mercy, and they give no quarter to those who exploit their tolerance and their indulgence.

'NO DEFENCE

'It is no use to say that the novel possesses "fine qualities", or that its author is an "accomplished" artist. It is no defence to

55

say that the author is sincere, or that she is frank, or that there is delicacy in her art.

'The answer is that the adroitness and cleverness of the book intensifies its moral danger. It is a seductive and insidious piece of special pleading designed to display perverted decadence as a martyrdom inflicted upon these outcasts by a cruel society. It flings a veil of sentiment over their depravity. It even suggests that their self-made debasement is unavoidable, because they cannot save themselves.

'This terrible doctrine may commend itself to certain schools of pseudo-scientific thought, but it cannot be reconciled with the Christian religion or with the Christian doctrine of free-will. Therefore, it must be fought to the bitter end by the Christian Churches. This is the radical difference between paganism and Christianity.

'If Christianity does not destroy this doctrine, then this doctrine will destroy it, together with the civilisation which it has built on the ruins of paganism. These moral derelicts are not cursed from their birth. Their downfall is caused by their own act and their own will. They are damned because they choose to be damned, not because they are doomed from the beginning.

'It is meet and right to pity them, but we must also pity their victims. We must protect our children against their specious fallacies and sophistries. Therefore, we must banish their propaganda from our bookshops and our libraries.

'I would rather give a healthy boy or a healthy girl a phial of prussic acid than this novel. Poison kills the body, but moral poison kills the soul.

'What, then, is to be done? The book must at once be withdrawn. I hope the author and the publishers will realise that they have made a grave mistake, and will without delay do all in their power to repair it.

'If they hesitate to do so, the book must be suppressed by process of law. I observe that the Irish Free State Government have published the text of their Censorship of Publications Bill. It proposes to establish a Censorship Board of five, four of whom must agree before any publication is placed on the Black List.

'Complaints must come through recognised associations, not from individual citizens.

'It may be that the establishment of a similar Censorship Board will be found necessary in this country as well as in Ireland. But our existing law is sufficient, if it be properly administered. Therefore, I appeal to the Home Secretary to set the law in motion. He should instruct the Director of Public Prosecutions to consider whether *The Well of Loneliness* is fit for circulation, and, if not, to take action to prevent its being further circulated.

'Finally, let me warn our novelists and our men of letters that literature as well as morality is in peril. Fiction of this type is an injury to good literature. It makes the profession of literature fall into disrepute. Literature has not yet recovered from the harm done to it by the Oscar Wilde scandal. It should keep its house in order.'

This long quotation and its predecessor represent the extreme points of view called into popular expression by *The Well of Loneliness* case. My own quotation roughly typified the standpoint of the witnesses summoned by the intelligent literary lawyers, Messrs Rubinstein, Nash & Co., to represent the firm of Jonathan Cape.

James Douglas's article – though few people would now deny that this was mainly a newspaper 'stunt' – stood for the other and far larger extreme, which unfortunately for Radclyffe Hall included the sanctimonious Home Secretary, Sir William Joynson-Hicks, and the Conservative Bow Street magistrate, Sir Chartres Biron. But for the appearance of this article, only a few intellectuals would have discussed a subject more or less ignored in England.

In 1928, sex phenomena were classified in two simple categories, 'nice' and 'nasty'. 'Nice' applied to love, marriage, legitimate babies and respectable romance, such as eventually led to the altar at St Paul's, Knightsbridge, or St George's, Hanover Square. 'Nasty' was reserved for almost everything else, and concerned itself chiefly with what Dr Kinsey calls 'the intolerance with which our Judeo-Christian culture views any type of social activity which departs from the normal'.

His Report explains: 'The general condemnation of homosexuality in our particular culture apparently traces to a series of historical circumstances which had little to do with the protection of the individual or the preservation of the social organisation of the day. In Hittite, Chaldean and early Jewish codes there was no overall condemnations of such activity.... The more general condemnation of all homosexual relations originated in Jewish history in about the 7th century B.C., upon the return from the Babylonian exile. Both mouth-genital contacts and homosexual activities had previously been associated with the Jewish religious service ... In the wave of nationalism which was then developing among the Jewish people there was an attempt to dis-identify themselves with their neighbours by breaking with many of the customs which they had previously shared with them ... Throughout the Middle Ages homosexuality was associated with heresy. The reform in the custom (the mores) soon however became a matter of morals, and finally a question of action under the criminal law.

'Jewish sex codes were brought over into Christian codes by the early adherents of the Church, including St Paul, who had been raised in the Jewish tradition on matters of sex. The Catholic sex code is an almost precise continuation of the more ancient Jewish code. For centuries in medieval Europe, the ecclesiastic law dominated on all questions of morals and subsequently became the basis of the English common law, the statute laws of England, and the laws of the various States of the U.S. This accounts for the considerable conformity between the Talmudic and the Catholic codes and the present-day statute law on sex, including the laws on homosexual activity.'

Thus Radclyffe Hall, seen in the largest perspective, was the victim of events going back in Jewish history to the 7th century B.C., rather than the

59

example of personal depravity that she appeared to James Douglas, whose knowledge of Judeo-Christian standards and their influence upon English law was likely to have been somewhat rudimentary.

* * *

Radclyffe Hall's book, dedicated to 'Our Three Selves', opened with a familiar quotation:

> ' . . . nothing extenuate
> Nor set down aught in malice.'

Lady Troubridge subsequently disclosed that this dedication, a subject of curiosity at the time, referred to Radclyffe Hall herself, Una Troubridge and Mable Veronica Batten. It was followed with a 'Commentary' by the pioneer sexologist Havelock Ellis – a pioneer indeed, for he was born in 1859, and published *Studies in the Psychology of Sex* in 1897. His work was known to few, and read by still fewer, for most of it came into the category 'not nice'. His introduction to *The Well of Loneliness,* written about 1927, raised no doubts regarding his sympathy with the author.

Forty years ago, except by a scientific few, the psychological variation known to us today as homosexuality was classified as sin, wanton and unashamed. Almost no one realised that its origins lay in glandular abnormalities, or that ancient history had any share in the condemnation reserved for them.

There was no pity for the acute nerves of the invert, created in the words of Radclyffe Hall by 'that terrible silent bombardment from the batteries of God's good people'. (The chief character in her book,

Stephen Gordon, is a courageous woman who wins the Croix de Guerre as an ambulance driver at Compiègne.)

'The crying need of our generation is for *insight* into the human nature, the behaviour of man,' recently wrote Stanley Cobb, M.D., the Bullard Professor of Neuropathology at Harvard University, in his foreword to *The Psychology of Women*.*

But in 1928 only the few sought to *understand*. For Sir Chartres Biron, the literary Metropolitan Magistrate; for William Joynson-Hicks, the Home Secretary, and for James Douglas, the militantly righteous editor, it was far simpler to condemn, and society as a whole followed their lead.

Radclyffe Hall, acutely conscious of injustice used *The Well of Loneliness* to express her own bitter feelings.

> 'An immense desolation swept down upon her (Stephen Gordon), an immense need to cry out and claim understanding for herself, an immense need to find an answer to the riddle of her unwanted being. All around her were grey and crumbling ruins, and under those ruins her love lay bleeding, shamefully wounded by Angela Crossby, shamefully soiled and defiled by her mother – a piteous, suffering, defenceless thing, it lay bleeding under the ruins.'

At this point in the story Stephen examines the locked bookcase belonging to her dead father, who

---

* A classic study by Hélène Deutsche, M.D., Associate Psychiatrist at Massachusetts General Hospital and a student of Freud.

61

had read the truth about her in volumes by Krafft Ebing and others, and who had loved and understood her.

'Then suddenly she had got to her feet and was talking aloud – she was talking to her father:

' "You knew! All the time you knew this thing, but because of your pity you wouldn't tell me. Oh, Father – and there are so many of us – thousands of miserable unwanted people who have no right to love, no right to compassion because they are maimed, hideously maimed and ugly. God's cruel; He let us get flawed in the making".'

'And then, before she knew what she was doing, she had found her father's old, well-worn Bible. There she stood demanding a sign from Heaven – nothing less than a sign from Heaven she demanded. The Bible fell open near the beginning. She read: "And the Lord set a mark upon Cain . . ."

'Then Stephen hurled the Bible away, and she sank down completely hopeless and beaten, rocking her body backwards and forwards with a kind of abrupt yet mechanical rhythm: "And the Lord set a mark upon Cain – upon Cain – upon Cain. And the Lord set a mark upon Cain . . ." '

The final passage of the book, with its anguished outburst of emotion, makes clear the invert's half-blind realisation that, though all passionate love brings agony as well as exultation, the agony of the love between two people of the same sex is unassuaged because it can never find fulfilment brought by the creation of new life. In the story Radclyffe Hall seems to see herself as caught in the trap of a pitiless society.

'And those terrible ones started pointing at her with their shaking, white-skinned, effeminate fingers: "You and your kind have stolen our birthright; you have taken our strength and given us your weakness." They were pointing at her with white, shaking fingers ...

'They possessed her. Her barren womb became fruitful – it ached with its fearful and sterile burden. It ached with the fierce yet helpless children who would clamour in vain for their right to salvation. They would turn to God, and then to the world, and then to her. They would cry out accusing: "We have asked for bread; will you give us a stone? Answer us; will you give us a stone? You, God, in whom we, the outcast, believe; you, world, into which we are pitilessly born; you, Stephen, who have drained our cup to the dregs – we have asked for bread, will you give us a stone?"

'And now there was only one voice, one demand; her own voice into which those millions had entered. A voice like the awful deep rolling of thunder; a demand like the gathering together of great waters. A terrifying voice that made her ears throb, that made her brain throb, that shook her very entrails until she must stagger, and all but fall beneath this appalling burden of sound that strangled her in its will to be uttered.

' "God!" she gasped, "we believe; we have told you we believe. We have not denied You, then rise and defend us. Acknowledge us, O God, before the whole world. Give us also the right to our existence!" '

The task of the scientist and sociologist is to find comprehensible and unemotional explanations for these blind agonies. In her recent study of female psychology, Dr Hélène Deutsche presents the French writer George Sand as a clear example of the conflict between feminine and masculine in some natures; she puts her forward as the classic type of man-woman who seems to carry a masculine soul in a feminine body.

'As a female,' Dr Deutsche tells us, 'her name was Aurore Dupin, and when she married she became Mme Dudevant. But her name that as a writer she made famous was her masculine name, George Sand. As a woman she led a very promiscuous life and ruined several men. As lovers she chose so-called feminine men, such as Chopin and Alfred de Musset. Each of her love affairs ended in destroying the man; her creative personality was split.

'If we assume,' concludes Dr Deutsche, 'that human beings have organically bi-sexual dispositions, that woman and man originate in a common primeval source, we are compelled to conclude that in the psychic economy of the individual, the two components, masculine and feminine, unified to form a harmonious whole. The feminine component should predominate in women, the masculine in men. When the harmony of the masculine and femine ten-

Una Troubridge when she first met Radclyffe Hall

Sir Chartres Biron

dencies is disturbed in an individual, an inner conflict arises.'

Recently Dr Sawle Thomas, Principal of the Princess Alexandra Psychiatric Hospital at Harlow, Essex, defined in conversation three types of homosexual women. The first, the simplest, is the constitutional lesbian who has no use for the opposite sex at all, and no wish to be other than she is. 'It is totally unfair to condemn this type, who is clearly made that way.' Radclyffe Hall's vivid description of Stephen Gordon's dumb horror when Martin Hallam, the good young man who wants to marry her, suddenly confesses his love, suggests that she herself belonged to this category, in which the expression of sexual desire provokes only terror and repulsion.

The second and more complicated type of lesbian is the product of creative and cultural factors. She is impelled towards homosexual relationships which represent a search for compensation and protection that could have been turned in the opposite direction. It is again unfair to condemn, since the impulse may have arisen from bitter experience.

Two homosexual acquaintances of my own are explicable in precisely these terms. One, a keenly intellectual woman with strong physical reactions, lost her fiancé in the First World War and clearly determined never again to suffer such anguish. From this only the total avoidance of heterosexual relationships would save her. The other turned towards women because, in an early love-affair, she became pregnant outside wedlock and clandestinely attempted abortion, from which her health suffered for several years. Being an individual of strong emotions, she found that she could get the satisfaction she sought in physical relations with other women.

The third type of lesbian may be described as 'environmental'; her emotions spring from family circumstances such as bad experiences in childhood. The quarrelsome relationship between Radclyffe Hall's mother and step-father may well have contributed directly to her own homosexuality.

A special inquiry into lesbianism by Bryan Magee, published by the *New Statesman* on March 26th, 1965, led to some conclusions which differed from those of Dr Hélène Deutsche and Dr Sawle Thomas. Bryan Magee tackled the topic comprehensively and, after reading the relevant section in Kinsey, questioning the organisers of the Minorities Research group, a lesbian society, and interviewing doctors, psychiatrists, sociologists, social workers and scores of individuals, he found he could reduce the number of genuine lesbians to somewhere between four and six per cent of the population. He also discovered (which he had not expected) that homosexuality is as common among women as among men.

He concludes that 'homosexuals are born, not made. Physically they are no different from anyone else. Homosexuality consists in an abnormal pattern of emotional development, such that the person is sexually aroused by, and prone to become emotionally fixated on – i.e., to fall in love with – members of his or her own sex ...

'What needs emphasising is that it is a question of emotional development, of personality structure. Homosexuals are not just people who indulge in certain physical practices. They do, of course, and they are responsible for what they do. But their physical practices are the expression of a whole way of feeling, of responding to other people, and this they cannot help. Being a homosexual does not, except for

66

a handful of borderline cases, represent a decision – one cannot, even if one wishes, choose to be, or not to be, homosexual.'

The writer comments that this is the hardest fact for many heterosexual people to grasp. They just cannot believe that the feelings between man and woman, celebrated in most of the world's literature and drama, in popular entertainment, songs, advertisements, are felt by some people in all their inescapability and strength towards others of the same sex.

He finds that there is no one thing that is always the cause of homosexuality; 'various causes operate, and they do most of their work in infancy. (There is a lot of evidence that failure to accept the child's sex is particularly important.) All this would explain why there is an abnormally high proportion of illegitimate children among homosexuals, and also of only children, and youngest children.'

Is homosexuality curable? If it is not, then the crass censoriousness of the Chartres Birons, Joynson-Hicks, and James Douglases is even more insensitive and wooden headed than it appeared to the witnesses of 1928.

'Most authorities believe that no cure has yet been found,' writes Bryan Magee. He states that the possibility in adult life is controversial – as, indeed, is the whole topic even today. It is clear that the intelligent layman has no alternative but to suspend judgment until many more discoveries about the mystery of human nature have been examined and made known.

We can, however, be grateful that the relatively sophisticated societies of today need no longer identify sex with sin. Free discussion of the human body

67

has come from many sources, which include the lessons now given to quite young children in school biology classes, and derives even from such casual and unscientific forms of information as strip-tease shows, identified by the majority with entertainment rather than knowledge.

At least we can suspend judgment and collect our facts in an unemotional atmosphere – something that, as *The Well of Loneliness* makes abundantly clear, Radclyffe Hall and her contemporaries could not achieve in 1928.

3

THE LITERARY STATUS OF
RADCLYFFE HALL

BEFORE *The Well of Loneliness* was published, Radclyffe Hall, who had written poetry from her earliest childhood, enjoyed a modest but respect-worthy reputation. Her poems carried such titles as *Poems of the Past and Present, Songs of Three Countries and Other Poems,* and *The Forgotten Island.*

The best and most successful of these early experiments, taken from *Songs of Three Countries,* was called *The Blind Ploughman,* and was set to music by Coleridge Taylor and Robert Coningsby Clarke. Its innocent verses run as follows:

'Set my hands upon the plough,
My feet upon the sod;
Turn my face towards the east,
And praise be to God.

'Ev'ry year the rains do fall,
The seeds they stir and spring;
Ev'ry year the spreading trees
Shelter birds that sing.

'From the shelter of your heart,
Brother, drive out sin,
Lest the little birds of faith
Come and nest therein.

'God has made His sun to shine
On both you and me;
God, who took away my eyes,
That my soul might see.'

Several famous singers, including Dame Clara Butt,
Chaliapin, Powell Edwards and Paul Robeson, sang it
as a powerful appeal for the wounded who had lost
their sight in the First World War.

Apart from these relatively undistinguished fragments, the only serious mental exercise which
Radclyffe Hall had undertaken was a succession of
spiritualistic researches, surprising in an ardent
Catholic, since the Roman Catholic Church had
always found such investigations obnoxious. The sympathy and advice of an eminent scholar-priest alone
made them possible.

Her interest in psychical research came partly from
the incentive given by the First World War with its
colossal casualties and the search for the possibility of

70

communication with the dead, but it arose more personally from the unexpected death of Mabel Batten. Oliver Lodge's book *Raymond* appeared about this time and Radclyffe consulted him on the technique of communication. His courteous reply led her to visit mediums and write careful reports of her experiences.

No revolutionary convictions resulted, however, perhaps because her interest was largely academic. Neither she nor Una had any friend or relative at the front, and hence the war's most poignant experiences passed them by. The chief value of this work, which left her with an open mind, was that it accustomed Radclyffe Hall to serious study, and trained her in methods of taking pains which later became characteristic of all her writing.

In an uncomfortable little house in Sterling Street, Kensington, off Montpelier Square, where she went to live with Una Troubridge in 1921, Radclyffe made perhaps her most vital literary decision. On a brief holiday together at the Lynton Cottage Hotel, they watched an elderly woman ministering to a wizened but domineering old lady who was obviously her mother. Radclyffe remarked in an undertone: 'Isn't it ghastly to see these unmarried daughters who are just unpaid servants to mothers who are sucking the very life out of them like octopi?' Suddenly she said: 'I shall write it! I shall write Heinemann's book for him, and I shall call it "Octopi".'

The disagreeable title eventually became *The Unlit Lamp,* which owing to its author's lack of literary experience took two years to write. Her reference to Heinemann went back to 1913, when Mabel Batten had discovered that 'John' had a brain. She believed she saw signs of talent in her short stories and decided

71

to show them to a possible publisher. This useful acquaintance was no less a celebrity than William Heinemann, then at the height of his publishing fame.

The result astonished them all, for William Heinemann wrote that the manuscripts were of high quality. One especially, entitled *The Career of Mark Anthony Brakes,* which described the sudden breakdown of self-control in an educated Negro under the stress of sexual emotion, struck him as perhaps the best short story ever submitted for his approval. But when Radclyffe responded in hopeful excitement, 'Then you are going to publish my stories, Mr Heinemann?' he made a reply which to her seemed extremely discouraging.

'I shall certainly do nothing of the kind,' he said. 'I am not going to present you to the public as the writer of a few short stories. You will set to work at once and write me a novel, and when it is finished I shall publish it.'

Radclyffe Hall was disconcerted and appalled. She had no intention of giving up her pleasant, easy life for one of strenuous literary endeavour, and seems not to have taken Mr Heinemann seriously. So she passed up the opportunity for which so many beginner writers would have given all that they possessed. By the time she began to think of literature as an appropriate profession for herself, William Heinemann was dead and *The Career of Mark Anthony Brakes* – an original theme when she first wrote the story – had appealed to other authors and failed to achieve publication. She had never been a regular worker, and was still quite undisciplined; she could not spell, or use a typewriter. Fortunately Una Troubridge was always available to read aloud from the untidy scripts.

A short potboiler called *A Saturday Life* followed the Heinemann episode, and two years later she handed to Newman Flower of Cassell's the manuscript entitled *Adam's Breed* which established her reputation. The scheme for the book first came to her while she and Una watched their obsequious waiter at a tête-à-tête luncheon in The Pall Mall Restaurant. Eventually she wrote the life story of a waiter who became so weary of handling food that he allowed himself to die of starvation.

If Radclyffe Hall had never written *The Well of Loneliness,* none of her three other better-known works – *Adam's Breed, The Master of the House,* and *The Sixth Beatitude* – contained anything to suggest her sexual peculiarities. All these books were deeply infused with charity and pity, and an unusual comprehension of every kind of under-dog, both animal and human. Their religious spirit is in poignant contrast to the supposed reputation conferred upon their author by pornographers and scandalmongers.

Adam's Breed tells the story of Gian-Luca Boselli, illegitimate grandson of Teresa Boselli, a tough, uncompromising member of a community of uprooted Italians living in Soho. Teresa's beautiful and cherished daughter Olga died at his birth without disclosing his father's identity. Teresa herself had married the mild, incompetent Fabio, who spent his time amid salami, spaghetti, and Italian cheeses of every variety. A naturalised Englishman wholly Latin in spirit, he sold his goods in a shop in Old Compton Street.

Almost before he could speak, little Gian-Luca endeavoured to express his pity for the slaughtered kids hanging in the local butcher's shop by repeating the inarticulate words: 'Oh, poor!', and finally by

73

avoiding the shop altogether. When he reached manhood he became a gentle lover of books and poetry, and started work as a waiter at the Capo di Monte in Dean Street. There he fell in love with his patron's beautiful wife, and here the author gives us a sensitive picture of the mind of a young man possessed by humble adoration: 'so tender and selfless a thing as to brush the very hem of the garment of God – a thing of pure giving, its motto was to serve.'

Eventually, partly owing to his good looks and attractive manner, Gian-Luca became head waiter at a smart Soho restaurant known as the Doric. He was most successful in his work, but gradually the food he took to the restaurant's customers began to nauseate and choke him. Finally he walked out of his London life into the New Forest, living 'rough' for several summer weeks, and there, amid the great trees which he had always loved, allowed himself to starve to death.

In dying he found the God of Compassion whom he had subconsciously been seeking throughout his short life.

Mr Newman Flower wrote of *Adam's Breed* that it was the finest story submitted to him in twenty years, but he did not think it would sell. Actually it sold twenty-seven thousand copies in the first three weeks. Published in 1927, it still has a small sale after forty years, and was translated into several languages. It was originally to have appeared under the uninspiring title *Food*, but the publisher insisted on a change, and it was Una Troubridge who eventually found a suitable name in Kipling's story *Tomlinson*.

The success of *Adam's Breed* was eventually responsible for Radclyffe Hall's conviction that she must write a book on sexual inversion, for which she

74

knew that she would never find readers until she had made her name. She realised that such a book could only be written by a sexual invert whose knowledge and experience would entitle her to speak for a despised minority. She recognised that such a book might mean the end of her career, but the conviction that she must do it became very strong, and after a discussion with Una Troubridge she decided to go ahead. She began the book in Paris in the summer of 1926. Much of it was written at the Hotel Pont Royal in the rue de Bac.

The Well of Loneliness tells the story of Stephen Gordon, the only daughter of a wealthy family, the Gordons of Bramley, with a country seat known as Morton Hall, near Upton-on-Severn. This lovely English countryside was now familiar to the author after her tenure of The White Cottage.

When the book opens Sir Philip Gordon, Stephen's father, is a tall and handsome man of twenty-nine, 'whose lips revealed him as a dreamer and a lover'. His young Irish wife, the Lady Anna Gordon, came from County Clare and married at twenty.

After reluctantly remaining childless for ten years, they found themselves expecting 'the fulfilment for which they had both been waiting'. Philip had visualised his wife only as the mother of sons; it had never occurred to him that she might have a daughter. They christened the unborn infant Stephen after the father's favourite saint, and discussed putting Stephen down for Harrow, or sending him to finish his education abroad.

But when the time came it was a daughter, not a son, that Anna produced – 'a narrow-hipped, wide shouldered little tadpole of a baby'. The parents concealed their disappointment from each other, and by the father's wish (though his wife experienced misgivings) had the child christened Stephen.

No brother or sister followed, and the girl remained an only child, whom her mother – a little outraged by her daughter's astonishing likeness to Sir Philip regarded with a strange antagonism. As though he knew by instinct that his daughter was destined to bear some unmerited burden, her father's adoration of her carried an element of bewildering compassion.

But it was not for some years that the reason for Sir Philip Gordon's instinctive pity for his daughter appeared. Stephen, only just grown up, found herself overcome by passionate repugnance when an honest young neighbour, Martin Hallam, fell in love with her, and asked her to marry him. In terror and repulsion she fled from him, and eventually asked her father to explain this overwhelming feeling of antipathy.

'Is there anything strange about me, father, that I should have felt as I did about Martin?'

The unhappy father could not face telling her the truth of which he was now convinced, and lied. There was nothing strange about her, he said – though the neighbours, who had never liked her, had begun to talk about her brutal repudiation of Martin, and unexplained tension produced unhappiness between the worthy parents. Sir Philip planned to tell her, but kept putting it off, until he tried, too late, as he lay dying after a broken tree had crushed him. But in the interval he had begun to read books, such as the works of Karl Heinrich Ulrichs, which seemed strange and shocking to that generation. These psychological studies would keep him reading half through the night, pacing up and down in anguish of spirit.

Stephen's own homosexual love affairs had now become numerous, with inevitably disastrous results. They began with her juvenile adoration of Collins, a pretty blue-eyed housemaid. When Stephen found the handsome new footman making love to Collins in the potting shed, she hurled a broken flower-pot at him in her rage and bewilderment, and thereby achieved the dismissal of both delinquents.

The next serious complication came through a worthless young woman, Angela Crossby, whom Stephen met owing to a dog-fight between Angela's small highland terrier and the local butcher's elderly airedale. Angela, the spoilt wife of a Birmingham magnate, was rumoured to have been on the New York stage. She was pretty, vulgar and cowardly, and Stephen fell deeply in love with her. To the comprehensible indignation of Angela's unattractive husband, she bought her a series of expensive gifts.

This first serious love affair, which seemed simple and natural to Stephen 'in accordance with the dictates of her nature', eventually created a situation which compelled her to part from her lovely conventional mother, and renounce Morton, her home. She began a new life in London with her former tutor, and painfully emerged as a talented writer.

Time passed. Stephen moved from London to Paris, and then came the First World War. She volunteered to be an ambulance driver and thus achieved a species of contentment, for in war-work even the invert can find a place. She was not a physical coward, and battles and bombs held no terrors for her. But her peace did not last. In the Unit she met and drove with a girl of twenty-one named Mary Llewellyn, with whom an intense love affair quickly developed. But Mary was not a total invert; she was vulnerable to normal heterosexual love.

Against the competition of such love the invert invariably loses, for all human biology is against her. Realising this after Mary had departed with Martin, (Stephen's former would-be lover), Radclyffe Hall breaks into the final passionate plea for justice, as she sees it, to which the whole book has led.

'She turned and saw him, but only for a moment, for now the room seemed to be thronging with people. Who were they, these strangers with the miserable eyes? Oh, but they were many, these unbidden guests, and they called very softly at first and then louder. They were calling her by name, saying "Stephen, Stephen!" The quick, the dead, and the yet unborn – all calling her, softly at first and then louder. Aye, and those lost and terrible brothers from Alec's, they were here, and they also were calling: "Stephen, Stephen, speak with your God and ask Him why He has left us forsaken!" She could see their marred and reproachful faces with the haunted melancholy eyes of the invert – eyes that had looked too long on a world that lacked all pity and understanding: "Stephen, Stephen, Stephen, speak with your God and ask Him why He has left us forsaken!"...

'Rockets of pain, burning rockets of pain – their pain, her pain, all welded together into one great consuming agony. Rockets of pain that shot up and burst, dropping scorching tears of fire on the

78

spirit – her pain, their pain . . . all the misery at Alec's. And the press and the clamour of those countless others – they fought, they trampled, they were getting her under. In their madness to become articulate through her, they were tearing her to pieces, getting her under. They were everywhere now, cutting off her retreat; neither bolts nor bars would avail to save her. The walls fell down and crumbled: "We are coming, Stephen – we are still coming on, and our name is legion – you dare not disown us!" She raised her arms, trying to ward them off, but they closed in and in: "You dare not disown us!" '

For several years Radclyffe Hall and Una Troubridge shared another Kensington house in Holland Street, near the Carmelites Church. This house was eventually sacrificed to help the legal costs of the battle over *The Well of Loneliness*. During these years police courts and lawyers alternated with life in a period cottage in Rye, overlooking Romney Marsh and facing the beams of the Gris Nez lighthouse. From the heights of the little town, the two carven figures above the famous gold-figured clock-face on the church tower recalled the vanishing hours, and reminded Radclyffe and Una that even the pain and humiliation of a public prosecution could not last for ever:

'For our time is a very shadow that passeth away.'

Actually, even at the time of its publication, *The Well of Loneliness* did not only bring humiliation; the

79

author's courage appealed to many non-lesbians who felt impelled to express their support in various quiet ways. One reader from Bristol, Jessie B. Heard, wrote a sonnet which expressed an admiration that lasted for over thirty years.

'Since Nature clothed her in abnormal dress,
Designed and fashioned of complexity,
Then she must wedded be to truthfulness
And of pretence be ever wholly free.
Deeply she loved. Uprightly she would hate
All cruelty, never for her the weak
Veneer of love, her heart protectorate,
Sheltered the unprotected ones and meek.

Rich was her spiritual life and strong,
Her perfect faith and courage was the sword
She held to wield with steady arm and long,
Her steel-like fingers carved the written word.

In all things brave, she did not waste or spend
Her time on fear. She did not fear her end.'

When the prosecution of *The Well of Loneliness* succeeded and the magistrate had managed to silence the witnesses who wanted to defend the book, Radclyffe Hall wrote another which deeply possessed her called *The Master of the House*. The inspiration for this story, which Naomi Jacob thought a greater book than *The Well of Loneliness,* came from a low stone archway in Fréjus which she saw as the birthplace of her boy carpenter, Christophe Bénédit.

As a convinced Catholic she undertook this strange study of the life of Christ as a young man with a conscious sense of purpose, and conducted herself with an appropriate austerity which was identified with a strange experience. Both she and Una Troubridge believed that she had been 'chosen' for the privilege of becoming for a time the bearer of the *stigmata*. Whether imagination or hysteria was responsible (and at this time the martyrdom which came to her through *The Well of Loneliness* was at its height), she was obliged to seek radiological treatment for acute pain in the palms of both hands, accompanied by an angry-looking stain which after some days of endurance gradually faded.

In *The Master of the House* the author portrayed the young Jesus, not as a Galilean carpenter but as a Provencal peasant, who as a conscript is ordered to Palestine in the First World War and there falls victim to a hostile patrol. Christophe Bénédit is the spritual brother of Gian-Luca who accepted death to save mankind. At the very end of the story 'he could hear his own stumbling choking words. They amazed him, they sounded very like madness, but a madness so sublime that his soul leapt and sang.

' "I, I am Christophe. I have come to ask your forgiveness. With these hands of mine I now bring you God's peace – the peace that passes all understanding. I have come first to you whom I have most wronged, but presently I will go out into the world so that the world may be healed by my message. In the name of Jesus Christ lay down your arms! He is here; He tells us to love one another, for our wounds are His. We are one and the same, and that one is Christ, and Christ is the Indestructible Compassion. God so loved the world that He gives Himself." '

But the starving, ragged Turkish patrol which had captured him did not understand his Provencal speech, and they spat in his face and cursed him and stripped him of his clothes. The small events of his life as a soldier paralleled events in the story of Christ. Finally his captors crucified him against the door of a barn, and as the embodiment of Indestructible Compassion he declined to defend himself.

'An unendurable pain in his hands, in his feet, an unendurable pain.

' "Lord, if You are with me still, do not stay ... do not suffer." '

But the words sank down and were lost in a bottomless pit of physical anguish.

'His head moved quickly from side to side as though he were trying to see his hands, to comprehend the cause of such suffering. Then it drooped as though he could see his feet and look on the rood they had nailed beneath him. But presently he became very still and his dying eyes gazed out to the East, where the flaming, majestic dawn rose over the world like a resurrection.'

It is difficult to identify the author of this mystical picture with the woman who was scorned and humiliated by journalists and politicians, and all who typified the Establishment. The two, one feels, could hardly co-exist in the same world.

Another publication, *The Sixth Beatitude,* followed *The Master of the House.* Hannah Bullen, the woman whose thirty-first year Radclyffe Hall describes in this novel, is a spiritual near-relative of both Gian-Luca and Christophe Bénédit; she gives her own life in the attempt to save her family and friends in their blazing cottage from a gale-driven fire on Romney Marsh. Hannah, like her spiritual predecessors, is a peasant, whose English is that actually spoken by the poor in cottage, field and inn. Her toughness is that of Teresa

Boselli, though Hannah is not an uprooted Italian but the very spirit of rural Sussex.

But by the time that Radclyffe Hall had created Hannah Bullen to join her gallery of remarkable and varied characters, the writer of *Adam's Breed, The Master of the House* and *The Sixth Beatitude,* was now inescapably the author of *The Well of Loneliness* and seemed unlikely to avoid her unjust fate of exclusive identification with the lesbian world.

4

THE CASE IS BEGUN

November 9th, 1928

EVEN IN summer, Bow Street Magistrates' Court, in the Covent Garden area of London, has a drably functional and depressing appearance. In November, 1928, and even more when the Appeal was heard at London Sessions the following month, the gathering murk of London's then smoke-laden winter cannot have had an encouraging effect upon the spirits of Radclyffe Hall and her supporters.

The part played by the firm of Jonathan Cape in this historic case began when Radclyffe Hall's agents, Messrs A. M. Heath and Company, approached them with the long manuscript of *The Well of Loneliness*.

The success of *Adam's Breed* had made her an attractive author to any publisher, but no one, in that day's climate of opinion, could have taken a story based on a frank presentation of the case for lesbianism without some apprehension.

When the hearing began the book had been out for only six weeks prior to its withdrawal, and had not therefore had time to cover its costs.*

If the hearing went against the publishers, the expense to them was likely to be heavy. But the sympathies of Jonathan Cape himself, a courageous, positive and liberal-minded man, were with the author from the start, especially after she had offered her own explanation. 'I wrote the book from a deep sense of duty. I am proud indeed to have taken up my pen in defence of those who are utterly defenceless, who being from birth a people set apart in accordance with some hidden scheme of Nature, need all the help that society can give them.'†

The hope that the courage and honesty of the author would help her book to survive the attentions of the popular press at its most ruthless, disappeared after James Douglas's sensational and biased attack on it in the *Sunday Express*. Fearing that a prosecution would be the consequence of this invective, Jonathan Cape wrote to the Home Secretary and offered to withdraw the book.

Sir William Joynson-Hicks, whom Harold Nicolson in the first volume of his *Diaries* called 'unctuous, evangelical, insincere', is best known to history for his

---

* The case was brought against the book as such, and not against any individual.

† Quoted by Montgomery Hyde in his Life of Norman Birkett (Hamish Hamilton, 1964, page 255).

connection with that Prayer Book controversy of 1928. It could have been expected that this sanctimonious Puritan would recommend the withdrawal of *The Well of Loneliness* as the best course. The publishers readily agreed and withdrew it, but Cape secretly sent the moulds to a firm in Paris.

Printing moulds are thinnish sheets of papier-maché made by first dampening them and then beating on to the surface of type until they retain an exact impression, as it were in reverse, of the type. Then, after being dried, they are used to cast stereotype metal plates. Molten metal is poured into the mould and so reproduces more or less exactly a printing plate which is, in fact, a reproduction of the original type.

In September, 1928, the book was reprinted in its original English text by the Pegasus Press in France under its own imprint, and published copies were then imported into England. These were seized, on the Home Secretary's instructions, whenever they were discovered, and accusations that the Government was indulging in a form of censorship became a controversial point of discussion.

Finally the Director of Public Prosecutions applied for an Order under the Obscene Publications Act of 1857 (popularly known as Lord Campbell's Act), which did not create any new offence, but gave magistrates throughout the country statutory powers to order the destruction of 'any obscene publication held for sale or distribution on information laid before a court of summary jurisdiction'.

'Thus,' writes Montgomery Hyde, 'as the law stood, neither the authoress nor, for that matter, anybody else could be called to give evidence as to the literary value of the book.'

The proceedings against *The Well of Loneliness* began before the Chief Magistrate, Sir Chartres Biron, a literary man aged sixty of conventional and restricted tastes. Apart from his career as Chief Magistrate at Bow Street from 1920 to 1933, he had no claim to fame. Mr H. F. Rubinstein, (Jonathan Cape's solicitor) subsequently described Sir Chartres in uncompromising words as 'the pathologically boorish magistrate', whose crude conduct seemed the worse because he was himself 'an author of some distinction'. He and James Douglas were precisely the same age, a time of life at which Conservative editors, magistrates and politicians are unlikely to modify their prejudices.

The Times report for November 10, 1928, confirms that Mr Eustace Fulton, the Senior Treasury Counsel, and Mr Vincent Evans conducted the case on behalf of the Director of Public Prosecutions, while Mr Norman Birkett, K.C., and Mr Herbert Metcalfe appeared for Messrs Cape Ltd, Mr J. B. Melville, K.C., and Mr Walter Frampton represented Mr Leopold B. Hill, the English agent for The Pegasus Press, of rue Boulard, Paris. The solicitors acting for the defence were the famous firm of lawyers, Messrs Rubinstein, Nash & Co., located in Gray's Inn. Two decades later they filled the same role on behalf of Penguin Books Ltd, in defence of *Lady Chatterley's Lover,* with a very different result.

For the prosecution Mr Fulton submitted that the theme of *The Well of Loneliness* was obscene, and said that 'a person who chose an obscene theme could not but write an obscene book'. He then called Chief Inspector Prothero of Scotland Yard, one of the 'Dogberries' instructed by the Director of Public Prosecutions, who gave evidence of the seizure of

87

copies of the book. Cross-examined by Mr Metcalfe, the Inspector said he agreed that the authoress had treated the subject with frankness and sincerity, but he regarded the whole theme as offensive because it described physical passion. He agreed that the book dealt with a well understood problem, but it was one usually discussed by medical men and scientists. Its literary and psychological subtleties were, of course, outside his field of comprehension.

'The book,' he reported, 'is indecent; it deals with an indecent subject.'

Mr Metcalfe then pointed out that the book was described by a critic in *The Times Literary Supplement* as 'sincere, courageous, high-minded and often beautiful'. 'Apparently,' he asked the Inspector, 'you do not agree with that critic?'

'I do not,' said Inspector Prothero; 'sincere and courageous, yes, but not high-minded and beautiful.'

Norman Birkett, K.C., then opened the case for the defence. He was the son of Thomas Birkett, a Liberal Lancashire draper with a business in Ulverston, and had served as an apprentice behind the counter of his father's shop.

In 1928 he had just turned forty-five, a tall, slim, spectacled man, with still vivid red hair, and a high forehead. He was never handsome but his tall figure made him impressive and he was noted for his beautiful voice. He was to die as Lord Birkett of Ulverston in February 1962. In 1946 he acted as one of the two British judges at the International War Crimes Tribunal at Nuremberg. A frequent correspondent of his was Morris Ernst, a well-known New York lawyer who successfully defended *The Well of Loneliness* in the American Courts with the same animation as Birkett had shown at Bow Street, and who shared his liberal views on literature and censorship.

Addressing the magistrate, Mr Birkett commented that Chief Inspector Prothero's evidence was a considerable over-simplification of the issue involved.

'The book is concerned not with perversion but with what the medical profession call inversion – that is, emotions and desires which with most people are directed towards the opposite sex, but are here directed towards their own.'

'Do you mean to say,' asked the magistrate, 'that it does not deal with unnatural offences at all?'

'I say not,' replied Birkett. 'Nowhere is there an obscene word or a lascivious passage. It is a sombre, sad, tragic, artistic revelation of that which is an undoubted fact in this world. It is the result of years of labour by one of the most distinguished novelists alive, and it is a sincere and high-minded effort to make the world more tolerable for those who have to bear the tragic consequences of what they are not to blame for at all.'

He continued by saying that the views of the critics had constituted 'a chorus of praise' from those well-qualified to speak upon matters affecting literature in general.

'There are in court,' he added, 'distinguished people who desire to testify that this book is not obscene, and hold that it is a misuse of the word for the prosecution to call it so.' Sir Chartres Biron then interrupted him. 'The test is whether it is likely to deprave or corrupt those into whose hands it is likely to fall. How can the opinion of a number of people be evidence?'

Birkett explained further.

'I want to call evidence from every conceivable

89

walk of life which bears on the test whether the tendency of this book is to deprave and corrupt. A more distinguished body of witnesses has never been called in a court of justice.'

The court was in fact crowded with the type of witnesses seldom seen in police courts. Their special qualities made the case unique, until the not dissimilar examination, of *Lady Chatterley's Lover* by D. H. Lawrence, twenty-two years afterwards. They included some of the best-known writers and intellectuals in Britain, such as E. M. Forster, Desmond MacCarthy, Storm Jameson, Amabel Williams-Ellis, V. Sackville-West, and Leonard and Virginia Woolf, who, not understanding the nature of the proceedings which involved no personal defendant, had generously agreed to go bail for Radclyffe Hall if the question of imprisonment arose. Bernard Shaw was sufficiently sympathetic to the defendants to come to a party given by Rubinstein, Nash & Co., for the witnesses at Brown's Hotel, but he characteristically declined to give evidence on the ground that he was immoral himself.

A greater problem than Shaw for the literary world was John Galsworthy, then President of the P.E.N.,* on whose support they had all counted. He refused to appear for the defence, and thus caused great difficulties for P.E.N. members, most of whom were in sympathy with Radclyffe Hall, and particularly for the Secretary, Hermon Ould.

Years later Mr H. F. Rubenstein wrote to me about the case: 'Thinking over what I told you the other day, I fancy I gave a wrong impression when I

---

* A world association of writers, founded in 1921. The initials stand for Poets, Playwrights, Essayists, Editors and Novelists.

mentioned that John Galsworthy was exceptional in refusing to help Miss Radclyffe Hall. The tone of his rebuff was the exceptional feature, but now that I think more carefully, the number of prospective witnesses we approached who declined to give evidence was greatly in excess of those who consented. I remember the feeling that popular writers (Anthony Hope comes to mind) almost with one accord made it clear that they were not going to risk their reputations by showing sympathy with an unpopular cause.'

After Norman Birkett's opening speech for the defence, he called Desmond MacCarthy, the Editor of *Life and Letters,* and asked him whether in his view *The Well of Loneliness* was obscene. But Sir Chartres Biron interrupted him.

'No, I shall disallow that,' he said. Supported by Mr Eustace Fulton, in whose opinion it was entirely a question for the Magistrate to decide whether a book was obscene or not, Sir Chartres continued: 'It is quite clear the evidence is not admissible. A book may be a fine piece of literature and yet obscene. Art and obscenity are not dissociated at all. There is a room at Naples to which visitors are not admitted as a rule, which contains fine bronzes and statues, all admirable works of art, but all grossly obscene.'

The Well of Loneliness, he added, had some claims to be literature and was certainly well written.

'I have to consider whether its tendency might be to corrupt. There are certain passages in it which, subject to exploration, appear to my mind to be obscene, in the sense of being lascivious and containing lurid descriptions of unnatural vice.'

Norman Birkett then formally tendered thirty-nine other witnesses.

'The evidence which a number of them would have

given is identical with that of Mr MacCarthy,' he said. 'In a second category are distinguished authors and authoresses who would have said that they had read the book and in their view it was not obscene. Other witnesses include booksellers, ministers of religion, social workers, magistrates, biologists, including Professor Julian Huxley, educationists, including the Registrar of Durham University, medical men, and representatives of the London libraries.'

But Sir Chartres remained quite unimpressed even by Professor Julian Huxley and the Registrar of Durham University. Irritably he exclaimed: 'I reject them all.'

During the morning Radclyffe Hall had sat silently in her place until Norman Birkett, briefed for the publishers, introduced a new plea that the relations between women described in the book represented a normal friendship. But in the luncheon interval she attacked him furiously for taking this line, which appeared to her to undermine the strength of the convictions with which she had defended the case. His plea seemed to her, as her solicitor commented later, 'the unkindest cut of all', and at their luncheon together she was unable to restrain 'tears of heart-broken anguish'. That luncheon, he added, 'was certainly the most miserable meal of my life.'

It was not less so because, in the course of the proceedings, he had come to entertain a warm respect and admiration for Radclyffe Hall, which surprised himself. He had begun by welcoming her 'in ignorant prejudice' rather half-heartedly as a new client for his firm, but gradually found himself liking her more and more, and becoming deeply distressed because, as the law stood, he could do so little for her.

Their respect was mutual; she was not the type to

indulge in resentment and recrimination against those who had unsuccessfully sought to help her.

'Even now,' he wrote years afterwards, 'when I read the words which she inscribed in my copy of "The Well" on the day after our final *coup de grace*, "To my friend ... from his grateful client", I feel humbled and shamed.'

Their friendship continued to the end of her life.

Reluctantly, Norman Birkett was obliged to change his position, and later asked the magistrate to state a case on the admissibility of the expert evidence he wished to tender. But Sir Chartres refused to state a case.

'It is open to the defence to appeal against my decision,' he pointed out.

Norman Birkett replied that, having regard to the Magistrate's decision, he did not think any useful purpose would be served by his calling any evidence. He submitted that the book did not offend against the statute, and could not in any circumstances tend to corrupt or deprave.

After Norman Birkett's colleague, Mr J. B. Melville, had also addressed the magistrate, urging that the book was a grave and reverent treatment of a medical fact and the problem which arose from it, the magistrate adjourned the case for a week.

5

THE CASE CONTINUED
November 16th, 1928

B
Y THIS time *The Well of Loneliness* case and its pornographic associations had attracted the attention of a large public, and especially of that smaller minority which is always conscious of the money to be made by the exploration of forbidden topics.

In spite of the still dominant Victorianism and pseudo-respectability of the period, clubs and societies existed where those believed to be specialists in the practices vaguely known as 'vice' were welcome. The greater their interest in sodomy, lesbianism, pederasty and kindred topics was thought to be, the more welcome they were as associates. Radclyffe Hall frequented one club known as 'The Cave of Harmony', where Katharine Mansfield gave amateur stage performances. Frank Harris was also a member.

The locked-cupboard atmosphere of these places gave them their attraction, and still does, in so far as they exist today. Large sums were paid for publications supposed to be 'shocking', and usually produced from the depths of a Bloomsbury basement.

According to Una Troubridge, a satirical booklet with dubious illustrations, entitled *The Sink of Solitude,* by Beresford Egan, gave the ladylike Radclyffe Hall considerable pain. This book, and another satire called *Policemen of the Lord,* in which the author ridiculed the puritanical Joynson-Hicks, brought Beresford Egan close to arrest. It was a risk of which he might well have been proud, since in its decorative fashion his lively pornographic booklet was a blow struck for liberty in the true Areopagitican tradition. One Low cartoon of this period showed 'Jix' as a nursemaid putting books on the fire with tongs, while children representing the public looked on ruefully from their cots.

Though they are still to be discreetly purchased today, the fascination of publications such as the Egan satire for a generation accustomed to the frank discussion of sexual problems is inevitably less than it was in 1928.

Nevertheless, there is still entertainment to be derived from the ingenious lampooning and the audacious Beardsley-like illustrations in their elegant white vellum cover.

Policemen of the Lord, A Political Satire, was

published by the Sophistocles Press and dedicated to Mrs Dora Grundy. Beresford Egan, the gifted unorthodox artist, still challenges convention from his home in Elm Park Mansions. P. B. Stephenson, the lampoonist and writer of the Preface, was a Rhodes Scholar and journalist, director of the Fanfrolico Press and, later, of the Mandrake Press (the first publisher of the D. H. Lawrence book of paintings). He died in Australia in 1966.

'According to the *Daily Express,* always a reliable guide to the sensational,' his Preface begins uncompromisingly, 'Sir William Joynson-Hicks, a Cabinet Minister, recently declaimed as follows:

> "The Home Secretary is a man who is exposed to every kind of attack, and he gets it very often."

'Well, here goes. The Home Secretary is asking for it when his public utterances are as provocative of contempt as the following piece of Ministerial simplicity:

> "It may possibly be that in the near future I shall have to deal with immoral and disgusting books."

'If this means that Government action is to be taken to suppress books dealing with sex "problems", Sir William is about to make a fool of himself once more; and the lampoonist will have to deal in the nearer future with Moral and Disgusted Cabinet Ministers. Greater minds than that of Sir William Joynson-Hicks have already been exercised upon the question of repressing the printed word, and the

96

conclusion which Sir William should make has invariably been: *Leave The Well Alone* ...

'Most literate people are of the opinion that the Holy Bible is "immoral and disgusting" in many celebrated passages; but no voice has been raised for the suppression of the Zenana Bible Mission, of which Sir William Joynson-Hicks is the Distinguished Hon. Treasurer. It would even be possible to find a great number of people to support the view that Traction Engines are immoral (anti-social) and disgusting objects upon the King's Highway; particularly that they are a menace to children. But no voice has yet been raised for the suppression of the National Traction Engine Association, of which Sir William is the capable President; and as yet no police action has been threatened against an eloquent pamphlet written by Sir William (perhaps the most distinguished fruit of his personal creative effort) entitled *The Law of Traction on Highways.* Let him once begin, however, the repression of books which displease him, and who knows to what lengths a future Home Secretary, with different moral prejudices, may go?'

The final page of the Preface suggests, in the last paragraph but one, that the author possessed the gift of prophecy as well as of satire.

'This is, above all, not a defence of *The Well of Loneliness,* which is a dull and insipid book. But for the combined efforts of James Douglas and Joynson-Hicks, the book would more than probably have fallen into insignificance already. But these two simple fellows, the one with his publicity, the other with his brief authority, have made almost a martyr of Miss Radclyffe Hall. Thanks to their crusade, millions of shop, office, and mill girls have been led to ask the furtive question: What is Lesbianism? It is probably a waste of time to point this out to Sir William. Let him proceed. He and James Douglas between them have made *The Well of Loneliness* a certain seller for years to come. I wish he would suppress this pamphlet, so that we could make a decent fight of it and expose him thoroughly.'

*   *   *

In the tense climate created by the clandestine controversies to which the case gave rise, the hearing continued on November 16th before the same galaxy of legal personalities.

Sir Chartres Biron delivered a considered judgment in which he made an order for the remaining copies to be destroyed and for each defendant to pay twenty guineas costs.

In giving his decision he said it did not seem to be generally appreciated that no question of censorship arose in this matter. The only question for him to decide was whether the book was an obscene libel according to the common law of the country.* He then referred to the important point on which Radclyffe Hall and Norman Birkett had differed.

'It was contended by the defence at first,' he said, 'that the book did not relate in any way to misconduct between women. Mr Norman Birkett drew a subtle distinction between what he called "inverse" and "perverse". He used the term "invert" to describe women born with certain masculine tendencies and with an inclination in certain directions which made them averse to relationship and intellectual sympathy

---

* As Alec Craig pointed out in *The Banned Books of England* (1937), he had to make this decision without any reliable definition of obscenity to guide him.

with the male sex; that in consequence of that accident of birth they were forced into intercourse – I use the word in its harmless sense – and into familiarity and companionship with their own sex which might very easily be misunderstood by a censorious world. Because of that, it was said, such people should be deserving of sympathy, and that an appeal for such sympathy was the purpose of the book.

'Having read the book,' he continued, 'I confess that I was amazed at the contention. I was not therefore surprised when, after the adjournment, Mr Birkett announced that he was not in a position to contend further that the book did not relate to unnatural offences between women in every sense of the word. But counsel for both defendants urged that the book in no way outraged decency; that the subject was dealt with with restraint and reverence, and that there was nothing which tended to defend these unnatural tendencies or to their glorification.

'There seemed,' he added, 'to have been considerable misunderstanding about the meaning of the word "obscene". It was contended that the book could not be described as obscene, because there were no gross or filthy words in it, and further, that because it was well written it was to be regarded as a work of literature, and not properly the subject of these proceedings. A considerable volume of evidence was tendered which, in my view, was quite inadmissible in law.'

He then turned to the conduct of the two main defendants, Jonathan Cape and the Pegasus Press.

'It is not without some significance that the two defendants who were available as witnesses in this issue have not been called into the witness box. It would have been a matter of some interest to explain how it was when Mr Jonathan Cape withdrew the book from circulation in deference to the opinion expressed by the Home Secretary, some of the seized copies were found in his possession, and some in the possession of the Pegasus Press. Upon that point both Mr Jonathan Cape and the Pegasus Press have maintained a discreet silence.'

'The proposition,' he continued, 'that the book is well written and therefore should not be the subject of these proceedings is quite untenable. I agree that it has some literary qualities, though these are defaced with certain deplorable lapses of taste. The mere fact that the book is well written can be no answer to these proceedings; otherwise the preposterous position would arise that, because it was well written, every obscene book would be free from proceedings. The mere fact that the book deals with unnatural offences between women would not in itself make it an obscene libel. It might even have a strong moral influence. But in the present case there is not one word which suggests that anyone with the horrible tendencies described is in the least degree blameworthy. All the characters are presented as attractive people and put forward with admiration. What is even more serious is that certain acts are described in the most alluring terms.'

Sir Chartres went on to quote extensively from the book. While he was dealing with a passage which, he said, described how some women of standing and position engaged as ambulance drivers at the Front were addicted to these practices, Radclyffe Hall interrupted. Abused, humiliated, the target of ill-natured gossip in all its painful varieties, she was nearing the limits of her endurance. With the magistrate's criticism of the much-respected colleagues with whom she had shared the perils of the war in France, she reached the end of her tether.

'I protest,' she exclaimed. 'I emphatically protest.'

Sir Chartres rebuked her. 'I must ask you to be quiet.'

'I am the author of this book,' she began, but was not allowed to finish. For the magistrate she was no different from any other delinquent being tried in that place.

'If you cannot behave yourself in court,' he asserted, 'I shall have to have you removed.'

'Shame!' she shouted from her seat at the solicitor's table.

Contemptuously disregarding her, Sir Chartres went on to conclude the hearing. He had, he proclaimed, no hesitation in saying that the book was an obscene libel, and that it would tend to corrupt those into whose hands it might fall. He made an order for the seized copies to be destroyed, and for the payment of twenty guineas costs in each case.

Notice of Appeal was given, although, as her solicitors have since pointed out, Radclyffe Hall had no chance of success as the law then stood.

CONTEMPORARY COMMENT

'Daily Express' – November 17th, 1928

Two hundred and forty-seven copies of *The Well of Loneliness*, the novel which Mr James Douglas condemned in the *Sunday Express*, will be flung into the furnace at Scotland Yard to-day.

Miss Radclyffe Hall, the writer of the novel, sat at the solicitor's table. She wore a tiny sprig of white heather at the side of her sombrero.

*   *   *

'Daily Herald'

George Bernard Shaw in an interview with the *Daily Herald* said:

'I read it, and read it carefully, and I repeat that it ought not to have been withdrawn.'

NOVEL CONDEMNED. MAGISTRATE ORDERS
'WELL OF LONELINESS' TO BE DESTROYED.
AUTHORESS IN SCENE.

Sir Chartres Biron, the Bow Street magistrate, yesterday ordered the novel *The Well of Loneliness* by Miss Radclyffe Hall, to be destroyed.

Defendants were Messrs Jonathan Cape Ltd., of Bedford Square, and Mr Leonard B. Hill, Great Russell Street, representative of the Pegasus Press, Paris.

Sir Chartres, in a long judgment, said he had no hesitation in saying that the book was an offence against public decency. He ordered defendants to pay costs in the case.

Points from his judgment were:

The fact that the book was well written was no answer, otherwise they would be in the preposterous position that the most obscene book would be free from stricture.

The way in which the Deity was introduced in the book seemed to be singularly inappropriate and disgusting.

Sir Chartres said there was a suggestion in the book reflecting on a number of women at the front, women of position and character engaged in ambulance work.

Miss Radclyffe Hall, calling from where she sat at the solicitors' table, said: 'I must emphatically protest. I am the authoress of this book, and I cannot let that remark pass.'

Sir Chartres: 'If you cannot behave yourself I shall have to have you removed.'

103

Miss Radclyffe Hall: 'It is a shame.'

Miss Radclyffe Hall interviewed after the case was ended said: 'Long passages in my book were mis-interpreted in the most amazing and shocking manner.'

'I particularly take exception to the magistrate's reference to the war work done by British women in the war. I defy anybody to read that portion of *The Well of Loneliness* which deals with the war work done by women and to find anything but the highest and most reverent respect for those women.'

Miss Radclyffe Hall's solicitors stated that the question of an appeal to Quarter Sessions was under consideration.

Mr Werner Laurie, the publisher, said he was shocked to hear of the magistrate's decision, and he hoped the Authors' Society would take the matter up.

'The Daily Mirror' – *November 20th, 1928*
Editorial

WHO DECIDES?

Who is to decide whether any book of the moment is to be suppressed on grounds of 'obscenity' or immorality?

We leave aside books of yesterday, and of old time, because it appears that age confers a certain respectability upon works of literature, or else that it is now too late to stop the harm that may be done by certain things in Shakespeare or the Bible, or in such classics as Fielding, Smollett, Swift and Defoe.

At present it seems that any indignant person may denounce any book, and that then a magistrate may say that he agrees or disagrees and let the book off or suppress it.

And if any number of eminent literary people, critics and novelists, ask to express their opinion upon what is after all partly a literary problem, they are told (according to law) that their views are not wanted, which seems to imply that all such persons are precluded by their profession from knowing anything about morals or taste.

Well, we must leave it at that, since, in the Twentieth Century, it seems to have been so left by law.

W. M.

'THE WELL OF LONELINESS' DECISION

'The decision of Sir Chartres Biron with regard to *The Well of Loneliness*,' says Mr James Douglas, 'is far more than a victory for the *Sunday Express*. It is a victory for good literature.' A victory for the *Sunday Express* the decision undoubtedly is; whether it is a victory for good literature, or for that matter, whether it is in the interests of society, we take leave to doubt.

It is arguable that *The Well of Loneliness* itself is neither a very wholesome book nor particularly good literature. Indeed, we should not be concerned to suggest that it is. It deals with a distasteful form of excess – and it handles its theme sentimentally, which is as distasteful a method of handling it as could well be found. Moreover, although there is not one word in the book which comes under the commonly accepted (which differs considerably from the legal) definition of obscenity, it does, in our view, show a certain morbidity as well as sentimentality in the treatment of its subject. At the same time it is obviously a book written with a purpose – if, as it appears to us, a mistaken purpose – and it is impossible to withhold a mead of admiration from Miss Radclyffe Hall for the courage she has shown in publishing it.

MR JAMES DOUGLAS'S ACHIEVEMENT

A society which came to have an intense, morbid interest in specialised and 'unnatural' forms of lust, or indeed any form of lust, would be in an unhealthy state, and we should regret to see the public absorbed in reading or our writers absorbed in writing books dealing with such subjects. But what, in fact, has been the result of the campaign against *The Well of Loneliness?* Obviously, as several of our correspondents point out, to increase public interest in it to a phenomenal extent.

Rumour has it that the first result of Mr James Douglas's article last August was that several hundred extra copies of *The Well of Loneliness* were immediately ordered by leading libraries. It is true that these copies have since been withdrawn from circulation, but it is also true that as a result of a protracted discussion on the whole subject there is scarcely an intelligent reader in the country who can fail to be aware of the subject which the book discusses, or who has not, as the result of the campaign, had his mind turned to consideration of that subject, whilst we are told that the booksellers in Paris and New York are doing a roaring trade. Between them, the *Sunday Express,* the Home Secretary and one of our Stipendiary Magistrates have succeeded, it would appear, in creating a world best-seller. It is a remarkable achievement. But is it exactly what they want?

THE ATTITUDE OF YOUTH

The plea that such books are bad for youth seems to us a particularly bad one. Children whilst still in the schoolroom can, as one of our correspondents points out this week, be better protected by their own parents than by the law. Whilst young people, once out of the schoolroom, always full of what Professor Gilbert Murray calls 'the normal and healthy reaction of youth against age,' take a quite especially vivid interest in anything that they are told not to read. It may indeed be said that the interest of normal healthy youth in vicious and unwholesome matters is almost exactly proportioned to the amount of trouble which its elders take to keep such matters from it. Who can fail to realise, for example, that amongst the first results of the suppression of *The Well of Loneliness* will be that surreptitiously obtained copies of that work will circulate immediately through every one of our Universities and will be devoured with avidity by many a student who, if it had pursued its normal unsuppressed course, could on no account have been persuaded in the course of a busy term to find time to wade through its five hundred pages.

THE NEED FOR A FREE PRESS

But even if it had been possible to secure the withdrawal of the book without bringing about that very concentration of the public mind on the subject with which it deals, which it has been the avowed object of Mr James Douglas, Sir William Joynson-Hicks and Sir Chartres Biron to avoid, it would in our view have been a mistake to suppress it.

The fact is that whilst there is much to be said for keeping our streets and shop-windows clean from pornographic postcards (whose object is clearly merely commercial) any laws which are stretched beyond this point, however specious the argument on their behalf, are against the public interest. We cannot allow our literature to be purged of all books which are unsuitable for leaving upon the nursery table. It has been frequently and correctly pointed out that in that case we should deprive ourselves of Shakespeare, the Bible – and Mr Bernard Shaw. It is true that if we reject the nursery table test we shall find the national bookshelves provided not only with

Shaw and Shakespeare, but also with a certain number of books which will appear to many of us – perhaps to most of us – to be calculated to do more harm than good. The result of allowing a free Press is that some things are published which contemporary opinion holds – and sometimes rightly holds – to be unwholesome and even vicious. Just as the result of allowing free speech is that every Sunday a number of Hyde Park orators make statements of which the mass of the general public heartily disapprove. But we have learnt to believe in free speech and (*pace* Mr James Douglas, Sir William Joynson-Hicks and Sir Chartres Biron) we must learn – or relearn – to believe in a free Press.

TREE OF KNOWLEDGE

A grown people must, for good or evil, be given the opportunity of making its own decisions. Doubtless some amongst it will on occasions make the wrong decision. In morals no less than in politics it is often dangerous to trust the people – but in morals as in politics it is even more dangerous not to trust them. The spectacle of the British Tree of Knowledge guarded by the flaming swords of Mr James Douglas, Sir William Joynson-Hicks and Sir Chartres Biron may be delightful, but it is scarcely one which a self-respecting nation can permanently afford.

(Not signed)

Sir,

I have read Mr Bernard Shaw's article on the Irish Censorship in your last issue. In Great Britain sex, as we all know, is the chief pre-occupation of the censor. Now, there are fifty thousand ways of regarding the strange fact of sex. At one end of the psychological spectrum is the man who feels that sex, and everything connected with it, is shameful; in the middle, the man who thinks of it from the hygiene point of view; at the other end, the man who sees in it the natural basis of a happy religion that praises life. One man is so modest that he drapes the legs of his dining-table; another accepts the arrangements of nature so simply that when somebody is put into prison for having taken a partial sun-bath in Hyde Park, he feels that he is living in a mad-house. Clearly, if there is to be any censorship of books, it is impossible to satisfy everybody.

The whole difficulty of controlling publication is the difficulty of deciding at what place to draw the line. I was surprised when, during *The Well of Loneliness* case, Sir Chartres Biron seemed unable to appreciate the difference between inversion and perversion; but I was not in the least surprised when he refused to hear the witnesses who had assembled in order to say that the book, in their opinion, was not obscene. Why should he hear them? If I had been on the bench, and if Sir William Joynson-Hicks and Sir Chartres Biron had gone into the box to tell me that the book was obscene, that would not have altered my conviction that to call it obscene is ridiculous. I should merely have frowned at them magisterially and have said: 'You find it obscene, and I do not; and as there is no accepted definition of obscenity, we are wasting time.' I know what I mean by the word. I should call a book obscene if it was manifestly written in order to make people think ignobly of the fact of sex; but obviously it is impossible to frame any definition of the word which could not be interpreted in fifty thousand ways.

The censorious party appears to be so apprehensive of the influence which erotic books might exert upon the young that they hope to reduce our literature to a library of Books for the Bairns ... a mind that is sufficiently libidinous can find, like the lady in the play, 'indecency in a hymn-book', and if our guardians intend to legislate on behalf of the most prurient members of society they will do an injustice to those who are not prurient.

On the one side we have persons who are anxious to save corruptible minds from being corrupted by books, although we may assume that such minds will always discover means by which to corrupt themselves. On the other side we have persons who find it intolerable that somebody should tell them what books they may read. A possible compromise between these parties already exists, I understand, in the practice of certain libraries. A librarian said to me the other day, 'That is a book we should put on our Blue List'. 'What,' I asked, 'is your Blue List?' 'Well,' he answered, 'we used to have complaints from parents that their children had taken this or that book from the library, and we now draw up a list of books which we do not actually expose on our shelves, but which can be obtained on request.'

It seems to me practicable to give up prosecuting a publisher for publishing a book, and only to prosecute, if that be considered necessary, a bookseller who sells a supposedly dangerous book to persons of unripe age.

Yours, etc.,
Clifford Bax.

72 Addison Road, W.14.

Sir,

Surely the issue around the question of censorship of books is very clear. There is a body of persons desperately (and quite genuinely) concerned about the morals of others. They can't sleep at night for thought of young persons going to perdition – and this preoccupation saves them from thinking at all about their own weaknesses and misfortunes, which is very happy for them.

This body of genuine crusaders is opposed by a rebellious nondescript crowd of immoral rascals who most perversely regard themselves as grown-up and object in any case to keeping the young too long in blinkers. They have an absurd notion that life is meant to be faced and experienced, whatever the risk.

Those who wish to protect and those who refuse to be protected – these are the two parties. There is everything to be said against the second party (composed of immoral libidinous persons) and nothing against the first save this: Experience has shown in a recent case that nothing flourishes like Taboo.

And it is a sacred thought for Messrs James Douglas, Joynson-Hicks and Chartres Biron to take to their beds with them that their united efforts have caused certain subjects to be discussed, inquired into and pleasingly investigated as never before in the history of this our hypocritical country.

Yours, etc.,
Hugh Walpole.

90 Piccadilly, W.1.

Sir,

There can be few people in the newspaper-reading-world who have not been induced, by headlines and posters in the streets, to read the verbatim accounts of the case *The Well of Loneliness.*

I had this book in the house and read it myself when it first came out, having a high opinion of Miss Radclyffe Hall as a writer. I realised that it was not a suitable book for my fifteen-year-old daughter, and without any fuss or difficulty I was able to keep it from her notice.

Since the first announcement of the law-suit in the Press, the daily newspapers have been filled with nauseous details, discussions and suggestions far more harmful than anything in the well-written book itself. The book costs 15s., the papers cost 1d., and for that 1d., instead of appearing in a quiet cover, they add glaring headlines and wide-spread posters. After reading the final summing-up, I defy any young girl or boy to remain ignorant of certain facts which ordinarily would never have come to their notice.

Is there no way that those responsible for the youth of this country may register a protest against the determination of the press to 'safeguard' public morality by this insidious campaign of publicity?

Yours, etc.,

A Modern Mother.

At Bow Street Police Court on Friday, November 16th, Sir Chartres Biron made an order for the copies of the novel, *The Well of Loneliness,* to be destroyed as an obscene book. On a previous day he had refused to hear the evidence of a number of writers of repute who were willing to give evidence in favour of the book. The order shows what powers are in the hands of magistrates and may usefully make the Home Secretary reflect that the sort of censorship he talked about would be superfluous. Attention may be directed henceforth upon the law as it stands rather than upon the shadowy project. As Mr Cyril Asquith points out in a letter to *The Times* on Wednesday, the law makes it an indictable misdemeanour to publish 'obscene matter', in regard to which the definition of Cockburn holds good that obscene matter is anything that tends 'to deprave and corrupt those whose minds are open to such immoral influences'. Shakespeare's Sonnets and *Venus and Adonis,* Plato's *Symposium,* the fragments of Sappho, and so on, all clash with the existing law. Of course, judges have steered round the law and protected the publishers of standard or classical works and of scientific treatises, but the literal sense of the law is unquestioned.

The decision in *The Well of Loneliness* case last week was a foregone conclusion. The blame for it – if blame there be – must rest rather upon the authoress and the present state of the law than upon the magistrate, who only decided as any other magistrate or judge in the kingdom must have decided in the circumstances. Sir Chartres Biron was certainly right to exclude evidence as to the literary merit of the book, since that had nothing at all to do with the question. It would be easy to name books of considerable literary and artistic merit – a certain book, for example, by Aubrey Beardsley, published privately abroad – which are obscene in an extreme degree. The question is whether the law can be usefully and effectively amended. It might be abolished, of course, and everyone be allowed to publish what they please; but short of that, we fancy it will be found very difficult to frame a legal definition of obscenity which will give the public what it wants and exclude what it does not want. In practice the magistrate must be allowed a pretty wide discretion. For our part, we should favour the tolerance of almost anything and everything short of the purely and obviously 'dirty', but if there is to be a censorship at all that goes further than this, then we do not see how *The Well of Loneliness* could reasonably hope to escape it. The authoress, it seems to us, made two mistakes; first, in writing the book at all – for people who desire tolerance for pathological abnormalities certainly should not write about them – and, second, in deliberately inviting the judgment of the Home Office upon her work. If she does not acknowledge the right of the civil and legal authorities to pass judgment upon a 'work of art', why did she have a copy of her book sent to them? If she had let well alone, it is unlikely that the police would have taken any action at all.

Here probably – that is, in what may be called the policy of the 'blind eye' – is to be found the only workable solution of this vexed and vexing problem of censorship. It is impossible to frame a satisfactory definition of 'obscenity' because a sentence which in one book would properly be described as obscene might in another book, written in a different atmosphere and with a different purpose, have no touch of obscenity about it. Yet this distinction is not one of which we can reasonably expect our judges and civil administrators to be fully qualified arbiters. We might be willing to leave the decision to Mr Justice X, but certainly not to Mr Justice Z. This being so the only practicable plan would seem to be to have a wide definition of legal obscenity – indeed to leave the law much as it stands – and to rely upon the administrative authorities to close their eyes to technical breaches of the law which are not forced upon their attention. That, in fact, is what they have been doing during the past few years. We could name any number of recently published books which would certainly have led to police prosecutions twenty years ago – when it was not even possible to publish a complete English translation of the classic *Mademoiselle de Maupin*. Now we have Ovid's *Ars Amatoria* in English! In short, apart from a few isolated absurdities, such as the searching of passengers' luggage at the ports for undesirable literature, the authorities have lately been behaving in this connection with commendable moderation and discretion. But if a book like *The Well of Loneliness* is forced upon their attention, what could they do but what they have done?   (Not signed)

116

'The New Statesman' – *December 1st, 1928*
Correspondence columns

'THE WELL OF LONELINESS'

Sir,
The attention of our clients, the defendants in the
recent proceedings, has been drawn to a paragraph
published in your current issue, in which it is stated
that Miss Radclyffe Hall made a mistake 'in deliberately inviting the judgment of the Home Office upon
her work'. The suggestion is, of course, completely
false. Miss Radclyffe Hall did not send a copy of *The
Well of Loneliness* to the Home Office. She was not,
as a matter of fact, aware of her publisher's decision
to take this step until she read an announcement of
the fact in a daily newspaper. We must ask you to
insert this correction in your next issue.
>
> Yours, etc.,
> Rubinstein, Nash & Co.

5 & 6 Raymond Buildings,
Gray's Inn, London, W.C.1.
November 26th.

(When we first read about this case we attributed
to the publishers the responsibility for having sent a
copy of the book to the Home Office. We were
subsequently informed that the publishers were not to
blame since they had acted on the express instructions
of the authoress. This letter makes it clear that we
were misinformed and we regret that we should have
done anything to further the circulation of an inaccurate version of the facts. – Ed. N.S.)

6

THE APPEAL

December 14th, 1928

THE APPEAL went to the County of London Sessions where the aged Sir Robert Wallace was Chairman. He now intimated that it would be 'neither appropriate nor practicable' for his fellow justices to read the book before hearing Appeal. The Attorney-General, Sir Thomas Inskip, K.C., Mr Eustace Fulton and Mr Bentley Purchase were present to support the decision of the Magistrate. Mr J. B. Melville, K.C., and Mr Walter Frampton appeared for the Appellants, Cape and the Pegasus Press, while Mr H. C. Leon held a watching brief for 'an interested party'. The Appeal was against the destruction order on the copies seized both from Pegasus' warehouse and from Cape's offices.

The fact that Mr Norman Birkett did not appear on the Appeal would seem to have predetermined its fate in the light of the course which was taken during it. It would have been known that Mr Birkett had appeared at Bow Street and that he had attempted to call literary evidence. Every Appeal to Quarter Sessions against conviction is a complete re-hearing. To the bare evidence of Inspector Prothero was added the devastating evidence from Cape's printers concerning the despatch of the moulds to Paris and the subsequent publishing of *The Well of Loneliness* in France. Because the type was identical in both editions, Mr Eustace Fulton was not only able to make telling comments at Bow Street about Cape's double-faced attitude, but now re-iterated them during the Appeal and gave weight to similar comments by the Attorney-General, who made it clear that the removal of the moulds was a commercial operation to save Cape's money, not to prevent the extinction of the book. Newspaper extracts confirm this.

Mr J. B. Melville called no evidence either from Cape's printers or Pegasus, nor did he call any of the previous witnesses. Together with Mr Birkett's absence, this made the Appeal a mere formality.

The Attorney-General, opening the case for the Crown, stated that the only point of significance was whether the book, *The Well of Loneliness,* was an obscene production. Lord Justice Cockburn, he said, had given the following test of obscenity: 'Whether the tendency of the matter charged with obscenity is to deprave and corrupt those whose minds are open to

119

such immoral influences and in whose hands publications of this sort may fall.'

He added that Lord Chief Justice Cockburn was dealing with a case which concerned the practice of confession, and said concerning the books in question in that case: 'It is quite certain they would suggest to the minds of the young of either sex or even to persons of more advanced years, thoughts of a most impure character.'

The Attorney-General then re-stated the facts in the current case. After referring to Jonathan Cape's decision to discontinue the sale of the book, he went on: 'It was plain that Jonathan Cape Ltd. then took steps to produce the book in France. It was produced by a company called The Pegasus Press and produced from the identical type, or moulds made from the identical type, used in England. Information came to the authorities that the book was being imported in considerable quantities into the country, or about to be imported, and they took steps which resulted in a warrant being obtained from the magistrate under the Statute and the seizure of a parcel of books numbering two hundred and forty-seven. A parcel numbering twenty-five was supplied to Mr Hill, a bookseller in Charing Cross Road, for the purpose of sale and distribution to the public. The French firm also circularised, to the knowledge of Jonathan Cape Ltd., a very large number of persons in the country advising them to purchase a copy of the book.

'The proceedings in due course came to the point at which it was necessary for the persons to appear and to show cause why the book should not be destroyed. The two parties who appeared were Mr Hill and Mr Jonathan Cape.'

Continuing, Sir Thomas Inskip said that, for all he knew, the book might contain very fine writing; he had nothing to do with that. The whole question was obscenity, bearing in mind the type of obscenity laid down by authority. He then described in broad outline the plot of the book, and said that the whole thing was meaningless except upon the submission which he put forward.

'I know', he added, 'only two references in literature to women such as those described. One is in the first chapter of St Paul's Epistle to the Romans, and the other is in the Sixth Book of Juvenal.'

The references quoted by Sir Thomas were as follows:

Romans I, verses 24–28
'Wherefore God also gave them up to uncleanness through the lusts of their own hearts, to dishonour their own bodies between themselves:

'Who changed the truth of God into a lie, and worshipped and served the creature more than the Creator, who is blessed forever, Amen.

'For this cause God gave them unto vile affections, for even their women did change the natural use into that which is against nature:

'And likewise also the men, leaving the natural use of the woman, turned in their lust one toward another; men with men working that which is unseemly, and receiving in themselves that recompense of their error which was meet.

'And even as they did not like to retain

121

God in their knowledge, God gave them over to a reprobate mind, to do those things which are not convenient.'

Juvenal: Bk. VI. lines 327–329

'Lenonum ancillas posita Saufeia corona provocat et tollit pendentis praemia coxae, ipsa Medullinae fluctum crisantis adorat in palma inter dominas; virtus natalibus acqua nil ibi per ludum simulabitur, omnia fient ad verum, quibus incendi iam frigidus aevo Laomodontiades et Nestoria hirnea possit. Tunc prurigo morae impatiens, tum femina simplex, ac pariter tote repetitus clamor ab antro "iam fas est, admitte viros"...'

Saufeia challenges the slave girls to a contest. Her agility wins the prize, but she herself has in turn to bow the knee to Medullina. And so the palm remains with the mistress, whose exploits match her birth! There is no pretence in the game; all is enacted to the life in a manner that would warm the cold blood of a Priam or a Nestor. And now impatient nature can wait no longer; woman shows herself as she is, and the cry comes from every corner of the den: 'Let in the men.'*

Sir Thomas Inskip was presumably referring to Juvenal, VI, line 320, and the following lines as quoted. This is, in fact, a description of a general orgy of which only the preliminaries were of a Lesbian character. Strangely enough he omitted any reference

* With acknowledgements to G. G. Ramsay and the Loeb Library.

to Sappho (circ. 600 B.C., the poetess of ancient Greece), a native of Mitylene in Lesbos, the name of whose birthplace is commonly used to describe the very category of women of whom Radclyffe Hall wrote.*

'It will not be disputed,' he commented, 'that the vice is an unnatural one, and *The Well of Loneliness* was a picture of indulgence in it. Therefore I would suggest that the tendency of the book is to deprave and corrupt those whose minds are open to such immoral influences – not the minds of robust and sane men or women who have a capacity for resisting such ignoble influences – and that it is certain it would suggest to the minds of the young of either sex, or even to persons of more advanced years, thoughts of the most impure character.'

The Attorney-General then read a number of passages from the book, and commenting on one remarked: 'This is more subtle, demoralising, corrosive, corruptive, than anything that was ever written . . . I hardly need ask what is the picture conjured up to the minds that are open to immoral influences.'

---

* Sir Thomas Inskip's statement that there are only two references in literature to female homosexuality is contradicted by the Kinsey Report (Chapter II, page 477), which states that for Ancient Greece, Rome and India, female homosexuality is recorded in the following passages: Ovid (First Century B.C. Roman), *Heroides,* XV, 15–20, 201 (ed. 1921: 183, 195, 'Sappho recounts her past loves); Plutarch (First Century A.D., Greek), *Lycurgus,* 18.4 (ed. 1914: 265); Martial (First Century A.D., Roman); 1.90 (ed. 1919, (1), 85–87); Juvenal (First-Second Century A.D., Roman); *Satires,* VI, 308–325; Lucian (Second Century A.D., Greek); *Amores* (1895: 190); *Dialogues of Cortesius,* V (ed. 1895: 100–105); *Kama Sutra,* of Vatsyayana (First-Sixth Century, Sansorit), ed. 1883–1925, 62, 124.

For additional account of Sappho of Lesbos, see Wharton, 1885, 1895; Miller and Robinson, 1925; Weigall, 1932.

Continuing, he said that obscenity must be judged by the standard of the laws of the Realm. The fact that someone who wrote a book did not intend it to be obscene did not matter. They might have the native of another race accustomed to practices which were part of religious ritual producing a book which would not be indecent in his or her own land, and yet he apprehended that in this country the Courts would condemn it regardless of the intention of the writer.

'I ask the Court to say that the book is obscene, having given my reasons without cloaking my language.'

Mr Melville then addressed the Appeals Committee. It was their submission, he said, that the book was a true work of literature and not a pornographic production. He quoted a number of passages from the reviews of the book, including the one from *The Times Literary Supplement* which described it as 'sincere, courageous, high-minded, and often beautifully expressed'. He did not think it likely that an obscene book would receive such treatment from the critics.

'There is no mystery or masquerading about the book,' he said. 'It faces the fact that there exists a class of women who are more attracted to their own than to the opposite sex, and considers the problems, reactions and situations which must arise in consequence.'

The subject, he submitted, was dealt with in a manner which could call for no complaint at all on the ground of indecency. The writer had dealt with the topic with more than ordinary restraint. Unless the Court was prepared to go very much further than the definition of obscenity which had been quoted, the Appeal should succeed. The book gravely and resolutely treated a human problem. It asked not for the approbation of an unnatural practice, but for understanding of the invert, and Christian charity for those whose misfortune it was to be differently constituted from their fellows.

The Attorney-General, replying for the Crown, said that certain passages quoted by Mr Melville might be above criticism if they stood alone. The whole book as to ninety-nine one-hundredths of it might be beyond criticism, yet one passage might make it a work which would have to be destroyed as obscene.

The Bench then retired, and after an absence of less than ten minutes,* the Chairman, Sir Robert Wallace, K.C., announced that the Appeal would be dismissed with costs.

In delivering this decision he said that the book was admittedly neither a scientific nor a medical book; it was a novel addressed to the general public which read novels. The opinion of the Court was unanimous. The definition which had been accepted for sixty years as to what was the test in regard to these books was whether the tendency of the matter was to deprave and corrupt those whose minds were open to such immoral influences and into whose hands a publication of this sort might fall.

'There are plenty of people who would be neither depraved nor corrupted by reading a book like this, but it is to those whose minds are open to such immoral influences that I refer. The character of the book cannot be gathered from reading of isolated

---

* It is interesting to compare the behaviour of the jury at the Trial of *Lady Chatterley*, in October, 1960. It was absent for nearly three hours, when the verdict 'Not Guilty' was announced, and was received with applause.

passages. The book must be taken as a whole. The Court's view is that the book is a very subtle book. It is one which is insinuating and probably much more dangerous because of that fact.'

The Chairman said in conclusion: 'In the view of the Court it is a most dangerous and corrupting book. It is a book of which the general tendency would be to corrupt the minds of the general body of those who may read it. It is a book which, if it does not condemn unnatural practices, certainly condones them, and suggests that those guilty of them should not receive the consequences they deserve to suffer.'

'Put in a word, the view of the Court is that this is a disgusting book, when properly read.

'It is an obscene book, and a book prejudicial to the morals of the community. In our view the order made by the magistrate is perfectly correct, and the Appeal must be dismissed with costs.'

CONTEMPORARY COMMENT

'The Evening News' – Friday, 14th December 1928

An appeal against the order by Sir Chartres Biron, the Bow Street magistrate, that a number of copies of Miss Radclyffe Hall's novel, *The Well of Loneliness* seized by the police, should be destroyed, was heard at London Sessions to-day.

Sir Robert Wallace, K.C., presided over a Bench which included two women.

Miss Radclyffe Hall, wearing a grey fur coat and a dark blue hat, sat at the solicitors' table in front of counsel.

Sir William Wilcox, the Home Office pathologist, and Sir Archibald Bodkin, the Director of Public Prosecutions, were also in Court.

The appeal was made by Messrs Jonathan Cape Ltd., of Bedford Square, W.C., the publishers, and Mr Leopold E. Hill of Great Russell Street, W.C., the representative of the Pegasus Press of rue Bouilliard, Paris, the printers of the book. They had been ordered by Sir Chartres to pay twenty guineas costs.

They were represented by Mr J. B. Melville, K.C., and Mr Walter Frampton. Sir Thomas Inskip, K.C., the Attorney-General, Mr Eustace Fulton, and Mr Bentley Purchase were for the Crown, Mr H. C. Leon held a watching brief.

The Attorney-General said the prosecution was based on the allegation that the book was an obscene production.

Messrs Cape, the publishers, sent a copy of the book to the Home Secretary, who thought it should be withdrawn.

Messrs Cape, in a letter, then said: 'In view of your decision we have no other course than to discontinue the sale of the book.'

Instructions were given to the printers at Frome in Somerset to stop the printing of the book, but to prepare moulds of the type which had been set up and to supply or deliver in accordance with instructions the balance of the paper which had not been used for the printing of the book. That was done.

Later instructions were given that the title-page and the fore-page were to be set up in type by the printers and moulds similarly made of that type, because it was not possible for the printers in Paris who had been instructed to print the book to set up type similar to that used in the type of the book.

'So it is plain,' said Sir Thomas Inskip, 'that Messrs Jonathan Cape, having written a letter to the Home Secretary, took steps to produce the book in France. It was produced by a company called The Pegasus Press.'

A PARCEL

'It will be proved that a parcel numbering twenty-five was supplied to Mr Hill, a bookseller in Charing Cross Road.'

Sir Thomas then outlined the plot of the book.

'Stephen is the heroine of it,' he said. 'The story begins with her birth, and the child from very early

128

years is depicted as a child with unnatural tendencies.

'The book deals with the friendship of this girl, afterwards a woman, with three persons. The first friendship is with a housemaid of the household.

'That friendship is but an incident in the development of the character of Stephen. The second friendship is with a woman called Angela, the wife of a man Raphael.

ROMANS

'The third friendship, and this is the culmination of the story, is with a woman called Mary. Eventually, the contest which leads to the conclusion of the book is one for the possession of Mary, between Stephen and a young man named Martin, who had fallen in love with Mary.

'The mother and father of Stephen are represented as deeply disappointed with the birth of a girl instead of a son, but the story is concerned not with the disappointment of the parents but with the character of Stephen.

'The mother of Stephen, as the book proceeds, is depicted as utterly out of sympathy with the girl. The time comes when the contrast is between Stephen's character on the one hand and the stern character of the mother.'

The Attorney-General said he knew of only two references in literature to women such as were described. One was in the First Chapter of the Epistle of the Romans, and the other was in the Sixth Book of Juvenal.

The Attorney-General read a number of passages from the book.

'What does this mean?' he asked of one. 'Imagine a

129

poor woman or a young man reading it. What is the picture conjured up at once? The man would ask: "What does this woman mean?". It corrupts him, conjures up a picture, which the writer of this book intends.'

'SUBTLE AND CORRUPTIVE'

Later, the Attorney-General remarked: 'My lord, some may think this book is corrupt because of the way it brings the name of God into the discussion of these passions.'

Another comment he made was: 'This is more subtle, demoralising, corrosive, corruptive, than anything that was ever written ... I hardly need ask what is the picture conjured up to minds that are open to immoral influence.'

'Unfortunately, all of us in the course of life acquire knowledge of human nature and of life which is sufficient to enable any of us to form an opinion as to obscenity,' Sir Thomas added. 'Obscenity must be judged by the standards of the laws of this realm. The fact that someone who wrote a book did not intend it to be obscene does not matter.

'The book seeks to glorify a vice or to produce a plea of toleration for the people who practise it. I do not know if it masquerades under the description of a medical or scientific book, but it is not in fact. It is propaganda.

'We have nothing to do here with the censorship of the press or of literature. For all I know there may be other books that are degrading. In this country we have a standard laid down by the law, and certain authorities have certain duties to prevent the importation and the publication from foreign countries of these books.'

130

Inspector John Prothero gave evidence of seizing books at various premises, including those of Mr Leopold Hill and Messrs Jonathan Cape Ltd.

Mr Melville: 'Are you also aware that after the customs had detained the books and after the matter had been considered by them, they gave instructions for the release of a consignment of the copies that had been seized?' – 'I know the police received instructions to release the book.'

Mr Humphrey Tanner, of the Frome firm which printed the book, said he was instructed: 'Please destroy any proofs you may have of the Paris title-page. Cape's do not want it to be known the type has gone abroad.'

Opening the case for the Appellants, Mr Melville said the book was exactly what it purported to be – a novel – and it was the submission of the Appellants that it was a true work of literature and not a pornographic production.

REVIEWS

He quoted a number of passages from reviews of the book including one from *The Times Literary Supplement*, which read, 'Sincere, courageous, high-minded and often beautifully expressed.'

He did not think it likely that an obscene book would receive such treatment from the critics.

Miss Radclyffe Hall had written two other books and for one she had been awarded a prize at the University of Edinburgh by Professor Grierson, when he occupied the Chair of Literature.

'*Daily Express*' – 15th December, 1928

Miss Radclyffe Hall after the case said: 'I would like to fight on, but I am advised that the question cannot be carried to another court. I was not exactly surprised at the decision after the way the case went before the magistrate at Bow Street, but I do feel most strongly that I as a serious writer have not been fairly treated. Neither has my book, as a serious contribution to a present-day problem.'

The '*Daily Mirror*' – December 15th, 1928

BANNED BOOK APPEAL FAILS
'DANGEROUS AND CORRUPTING', SAYS SESSIONS CHAIRMAN.
'SUBTLE THEME'. DEFENCE PLEA THAT PROBLEM HAS BEEN REVERENTLY TREATED.

Sir Robert Wallace, K.C., and a Bench of about twenty Justices heard the appeal regarding Miss Radclyffe Hall's book, *The Well of Loneliness,* at London Sessions yesterday.

The appellants were Messrs Jonathan Cape Ltd., the publishers, and Mr Leopold R. Hill of Gt. Russell Street, W.C., the representative of The Pegasus Press, of Paris, the printers of the book.

The appeal was against the decision that copies of the book seized by the police be destroyed on the ground that the book was obscene.

Mr Rudyard Kipling sat behind counsel, and amongst others present were Dr Marie Stopes and Sir William Wilcox.

Sir T. Inskip, K.C., the Attorney-General, said the prosecution was based on the allegation that the book was an obscene production.

It was published by the reputable firm of Jonathan Cape, who, in consequence of some attention having been drawn to the book, sent a copy to the Home Secretary, apparently for his opinion.

The Home Secretary expressed the view that the book was obscene and expected that it would be withdrawn from publication.

The firm replied that in view of the Home Secretary's decision they had no other course but to discontinue the printing and sale of the book.

PRINTING IN PARIS

What happened was that instructions were given to the printers at Frome, in Somerset, to stop printing the book, but to prepare moulds of the type which had been set up.

The title page was set up and the moulds were made. It would not have been possible for the printers in Paris, who had been instructed to produce the book, to set up type similar to that used in the body of the book, and it was quite plain that after Messrs Jonathan Cape had written the letter to the Home Secretary they were taking steps to produce the book in France.

It was produced there by a company called The Pegasus Press and produced undoubtedly from identical type moulds.

When information came to the authorities that the book was being imported in considerable quantities into this country they took steps which resulted in the warrant being obtained and the seizure of two hundred and forty-seven copies in the hands of Mr Hill.

PASSAGES QUOTED

Counsel dealt at length with the story in the book, which he said, presented the life of a girl named Stephen, whom he supposed he might describe as the heroine.

She was a girl born out of her physical sphere and he traced her friendships with a servant in her parents' household and two other women.

He quoted numerous passages from the book and submitted that the tendency was to deprave and corrupt those whose minds were open to unnatural influence.

'It is not a medical or scientific book,' he added. 'I don't know whether it masquerades as being medical or scientific, but no description could make it either a medical or a scientific book. I submit it is propaganda pure and simple.'

WORK OF LITERATURE

Mr J. B. Melville, K.C., for the appellants, said the submission was that the book was a true work of literature.

Counsel said that at the police court they had some dozen witnesses who were prepared to give their views upon the worth, the value and the decency of the book. That evidence, however, was excluded.

'I have searched the book from end to end,' said counsel, 'to see if I could find any passages that might be considered coarse. I have failed to find any.'

134

'This is a grave treatment and reverent treatment of a human problem which exists.'

In giving the decision of the Court, Sir Robert Wallace said there were plenty of people who would not be depraved or corrupted by reading this book, but there were also those whose minds were open to such immoral influence.

'The view of this Court is that this book is very subtle, insinuating in the theme it propounds, and much more dangerous because of that fact.'

'It is the view of this Court that this is a most dangerous and corrupting book . . . that it is a disgusting book, that it is an obscene book, a book which is prejudicial to the morals of the community, and in our view the order made by the magistrate was a fair one, and the appeal is dismissed with costs.'

THE BANNED BOOK
Well of Loneliness APPEAL FAILS.
'SUBTLE AND CORRUPTIVE,' SAYS ATTORNEY-GENERAL.

Fashionably dressed in a grey fur coat and dark blue hat, Miss Radclyffe Hall, the authoress, heard a Bench of magistrates at London Sessions reject the appeal against an order by Sir Chartres Biron at Bow Street, that the seized copies of her novel, *The Well of Loneliness,* should be destroyed on the ground of obscenity.

The Attorney-General, Sir Thomas Inskip, K.C., in an explanation of the facts of the prosecution and the present appeal, outlined the plot of the book. 'Stephen is the heroine of it,' he said. 'The story begins at her birth, and the child from very early years is depicted as a child with unnatural tendencies. The book deals with the friendship of this girl, afterwards a woman, with three persons. The first friendship is with a maid in the household. That friendship is but an incident in the development of the character of Stephen. The second friendship is with a woman called Angela, wife of a man Raphael. The third friendship, and this is the culmination of the story, is with a woman called Mary. The contest which leads to the conclusion of the book is one for the possession of Mary, between Stephen and a young man named Martin, who had fallen in love with Mary.

'The mother and father of Stephen are represented as deeply disappointed with the birth of a girl instead of a son, but the story is concerned not with the

136

disappointment of the parents but with the character of Stephen. The mother of Stephen, as the book proceeds, is depicted as utterly out of sympathy with the girl. The time comes when the contrast is between Stephen's character on the one hand and the stern character of the mother on the other.' – The Attorney-General knew of only

TWO REFERENCES IN LITERATURE

to women such as were described. One was in the First Chapter of the Epistle to the Romans, and the other in the Sixth Book of Juvenal. 'My Lord,' exclaimed the Attorney-General, 'some may think this book is corrupt because of the way it brings the name of God into the discussion of these passions.' Another comment he made was:

THIS IS MORE SUBTLE, DEMORALISING, CORROSIVE, CORRUPTIVE, THAN ANYTHING THAT WAS EVER WRITTEN . . .

In giving the Court's decision, Sir Robert Wallace remarked: 'The definition which has been accepted for sixty years as to what is the test in regard to these books is whether the tendency of the matter is to deprave and corrupt those whose lives are open to such immoral influences, and into whose hands a publication of this sort may fall. There are plenty of people who would be neither depraved nor corrupted by reading a book like this. But it is to those whose minds are open to such immoral influences that I refer. The character of the book cannot be gathered from the reading of isolated passages. They give an indication as to the general tendency, but the book must be taken as a whole. The view of the Court is that this book is a very subtle work. It is one which is insinuating and probably more dangerous because of that fact. In the view of the Court it is a most dangerous and corrupting book. It is a book which, if it does not commend unnatural practices, certainly condones them, and suggests that those guilty of them should not receive the consequences they deserve to suffer. Put in a word, the view of this Court is that this is a disgusting book when properly read. It is an obscene book, and a book prejudicial to the morals of the community. In our view the order made by the magistrate is perfectly correct, and the appeal must be dismissed with costs.'

7

THE AMERICAN TRIAL

April 8th, 1929

'*The People of the State of New York versus
Donald Friede and Covici-Friede.*'

'*At the very heart of the censorship tangle lies the
question of freedom — freedom to create in fidelity to
the artist's vision and freedom to share in the vision of
the artist if we choose. Almost every great literary
artist has been frowned on or frozen out by some
official censor at some time or another — precisely
because the artist is an eye among the blind, most of
whom think darkness light enough.*'

*Philip Scharfer,
Introduction to* 'Censorship:
The Search for the Obscene',
*By Morris L. Ernst and Alan
U. Schwartz.*

139

THE AMERICAN case against *The Well of Loneliness* began when P. Covici and D. S. Friede published the book on December 15th, 1928. In less than a month more than 20,000 copies had been sold, and the sales were reaching the top of the best-seller list.

On January 22, 1929, two copies of *The Well of Loneliness* were given to Magistrate Hyman Bushel of the West Side Court, and Donald Friede, Vice-President of Covici-Friede, was arraigned on a summons obtained by John S. Sumner, Secretary of the New York Society for the Suppression of Vice. Mr Friede and his firm were charged with violation of Section 1141 of the penal law, 'relating to the circulation of indecent literature'.

'The book,' added the *New York Times* in reporting the case, 'was recently declared obscene by the English Courts.' Mr Sumner, who was the only witness, testified that he had bought a copy of the book for $5, and the previous Friday, after obtaining search warrants from Chief Magistrate McAdoo, he and two policemen seized eight hundred and sixty-five copies of the work at the publisher's offices. His action, he maintained, was taken as a result of complaints received by his Society. Magistrate Bushel deferred further hearing of the case until February 5th in the Tombs Court, to allow time for his examination of the book.

The case was tried in the Court of Special Sessions of the City of New York on April 8th, 1929, and was listed as 'The People of the State of New York versus Donald Friede and Covici-Friede, Inc.' The court's decision was deferred to April 19th. The lawyers concerned were the well-known New York firm of Greenbaum, Wolff and Ernst.

To support his contention that *The Well of Loneliness* was not obscene, Mr Morris Ernst, attorney for the publishers, brought letters and telegrams of protest from prominent authors and psychiatrists against Mr Sumner's efforts to suppress the book. These, however, were not offered in evidence. The lawyers' statement of the case began with the words: 'The defendants were tried in this court on April 8th, 1929, having made no application for a jury trial, charged with the prosecution and sale of a publication called *The Well of Loneliness* alleged in the information to be a certain 'obscene, lewd, lascivious and disgusting book'.

This information might appear to be the simple and straight-forward report of a police-court case, but owing to the lapse of forty years the details were not easy for an English investigator to discover. Nevertheless, I received most excellent and intelligent assistance from the Law Library of the University of Illinois, whose officials investigated the case for me, and discovered, with the help of colleagues at the School of Law Library, New York University, that the transcript of the trial which I had hoped to obtain was no longer available because the Court of Special Sessions 'is not one of record', and its early records, which included this case, were destroyed twenty years ago.

They went on to say: 'All that can be procured from this Court is a certification as the disposition of the case – not of the trial record.' They concluded, however, that the Court 'apparently dismissed the indictment against the defendants' – a contrary result to that obtained in England.

A further discovery was the text of the statement made in the Magistrate's Court City of New York, on

February 21st, 1929, by the City Magistrate Judge Hyman Bushel, sitting without a jury. His opinion of *The Well of Loneliness* was clearly no more favourable than that of his British counterpart, Sir Chartres Biron, but he did not arguably exceed his magisterial function by suppressing the evidence. His published 'opinion' contained the following passages:

'The book here involved is a novel dealing with the childhood and early womanhood of a female invert. In broad outline the story shows how these unnatural tendencies manifested themselves from early childhood; the queer attraction of the child to the maid in the household; her affairs with one Angela Crossby, a normally sexed but unhappily married woman, causing further dissension between the latter and her husband; her jealousy of another man who later debauched this married woman, and her despair, in being supplanted by him in Angela's affections, are vividly portrayed.

'The book culminates with an extended elaboration upon her intimate relations with a normal young girl, who becomes a helpless subject of her perverted influence and passion and pictures the struggle of this girl's affections between this invert and a man from whose normal advances she herself had previously recoiled, because of her own perverted nature. Her sex experiences are set forth in some detail, and also her visits to various resorts frequented by male and female inverts.

'The author has treated these incidents

not without some restraint nor is it disputed that the book has literary merits. To quote the People's brief: "It is a well-written, carefully constructed piece of fiction and contains no unclean words." Yet the narrative does not veer from its central theme and the emotional and literary setting in which they are found give the incidents described therein great force and poignancy. The unnatural and depraved relationships portrayed are sought to be idealised and extolled. The characters in the book who indulge in these vices are described in attractive terms and it is maintained throughout that they be accepted on the same plane as persons normally constituted and that their perverse and inverted love is as worthy as the affection between normal beings, and should be considered just as sacred by society.'

ommenting on this opinion in their classic study *sorship: The Search For the Obscene*, which s eight pages to *The Well of Loneliness* case, Morris rnst and Alan U. Schwartz remark: 'We assume the good judge might have concluded that the was legal if Radclyffe Hall, the author, had had characters apologetic for what they did to life and t life did to them.'

Judge Bushel continued: 'The book can have no moral values since it seems to justify the right of a pervert to prey upon normal members of a community and to uphold such relationship as noble and lofty. Although it pleads for tolerance on the part of society of those possessed of and inflicted with perverted traits and tendencies, it does not argue for repression or moderation of insidious impulses. An idea of the moral tone which the book assumes may be gained from the attitude taken by its principal character towards her mother, pictured as a harsh, cruel and pitiless woman because of the abhorrence she displays to unnatural lust and to whom, because of that reaction, the former says: "But what I will never forgive is your daring to try and make me ashamed of my love. I'm not ashamed of it, there's no shame in me."

'The theme of the novel is not only anti-social and offensive to public morals and decency, but the method in which it is developed, in its highly emotional way, attracting and focusing attention upon perverted ideas and unnatural vices, and seeking to justify and idealise them, is strongly calculated to corrupt and debase those members of the community who would be susceptible to its immoral influence.

'I am convinced that *The Well of Loneliness* tends to debauch public morals, that its subject matter is offensive to public decency and that it is calculated to deprave and corrupt minds open to its immoral influences and who might come in contact with it, and applying the rules and recognised standards of interpretation as laid down by our courts, I refuse to hold as matter of law that the book in question is not violative of the Statute. Accordingly, and under the stipulation entered into in this case, that the testimony taken upon the summons shall be the testimony taken upon the complaint if one is ordered, I hereby order a complaint against these defendants. The motion to dismiss the complaint is denied, and these defendants are held for the action of the Court of Special Sessions.'

In spite of this formidable adverse opinion and the decision to which it led, the subsequent dismissal of the case against the defendants was clearly due to their admirably prepared brief and the fact that this brilliant document, which ran to fifty-one pages, was duly considered by the court. It began by directing the Court's attention to the significant fact that in recent years 'there has not been a single instance where a book, modern or classic, which was first generally accepted by the press, literary critics, the reading public and the community at large, and which was openly dealt with by the publishers and the book trade, was ultimately condemned by the courts, even though criminal prosecution was instigated at the outset by the same complainant as in this case.'

After comparing *The Well of Loneliness* with similar books, such as Theophile Jantier's *Mademoiselle de Maupin* and *Madeleine*, the autobiography of a prostitute (both cleared by the courts of New York State), the defendants continued: 'This is, in essence, a test case. It has none of the tell-tale characteristics of the usual obscenity prosecution. In the past the courts have shown no hesitation in suppressing pornography and in visiting punishment

145

on purveyors of filth surreptitiously distributed. But the courts have just as definitely declined to extend their ban to the literary works of authors of integrity and reputation acclaimed by men of letters and by the public. In this case there have been no elements of stealth or sly furtiveness, no suspicious or disreputable circumstances, no indicia such as customarily betray the spreaders of corrupt material. A sincere, serious, beautiful book has been fearlessly published and disseminated. The question is whether this court will now renounce the enlightened policy expressed in our recent cases, brand it as obscene, and open the door henceforth to the wanton and undiscerning prosecution of legitimate literature.'

The defendants went on to contend that *The Well of Loneliness* was not obscene according to the definition of obscenity that had been formulated by the courts; that on the contrary it was a distinguished novel of social value and significance. 'The test of obscenity is a living standard and any book must be judged by the mores of the day.' They then made, and skilfully explained, the following seven points:

(1) *The Well of Loneliness* is not obscene according to the definitions of obscenity that have been laid down by the courts;
(2) In the light of the cases involving *Madeleine* and *Mademoiselle de Maupin,* both cleared by the courts of this state, *The Well of Loneliness* must likewise be held free from obscenity;
(3) The circumstances surrounding the publication and the sale of *The Well of Loneliness* negate and refute any implication of obscenity;

146

(4) The test of obscenity is a living standard and any book must be judged by the mores of the day;

(5) All cases where suppression has been judicially upheld involved elements utterly alien to the book before the court, and are clearly distinguishable therefrom;

(6) In judging *The Well of Loneliness* by the long established rules, it must be read as a whole; and on that basis it must be upheld;

(7) The information should be dismissed and the defendants acquitted.

The skilled arguments of the defendants were sustained by statements from eminent doctors, clergy and critics, who included such personalities as Dr Joseph Collins, Boris Sokoloff (Professor of Psychology), Sinclair Lewis, Ernest Sutherland Bates, Edna Ferber and Rabbi Felix H. Levy. A further list followed of 'a few of the distinguished men of letters, educators, publishers, artists and publicists that have protested against the suppression of *The Well of Loneliness*.' Among the 74 names that followed were those of Sherwood Anderson, William Rose Benet, John Dos Passos, Theodore Dreiser, Ernest Hemingway, Robert Northan, Upton Sinclair, Lincoln Steffens, Carl Van Doren, Mark Van Doren and James Branch Cabell.

This clear and exhaustive treatment of the subject had its effect and might well have been put forward by the British magistrates as an example of the way in which similar cases should be conducted.

The final result was announced on April 20, 1929, by the *New York Times*:

* * *

'Well of Loneliness' Cleared in Courts Here.

'Justices Solomon, Healy and McIneriney in Special Sessions declared yesterday the book, *The Well of Loneliness,* by Miss Radclyffe Hall, the English writer, although dealing with "a delicate social problem", was not published and sold in this city in violation of the law against objectionable literatures.

'The court therefore discharged Donald Friede, President of the Covici-Friede Corporation . . . and quashed the charge against the Corporation made by John S. Sumner, Secretary of the Society for the Suppression of Vice.'

Only the previous day, Mr Friede had been convicted by a jury in Boston of violating the Massachusetts Statute against objectionable literature by his distribution there of Theodore Dreiser's *An American Tragedy.* The sentence in that case was deferred until June 1st, and he hurried to New York to be present at the rendering of the decision regarding *The Well of Loneliness.*

The court's decision said: 'The book in question deals with a delicate social problem which, in itself, cannot be said to be in violation of the law unless it is written in such a manner as to make it obscene . . . and tends to deprave and corrupt minds open to immoral influences.

'This is a criminal prosecution and, as judges of the facts and the law, we are not called upon, nor is it within our province, to recommend or advise against the reading of any book, nor is it within our province to pass an opinion as to the merits or demerits thereof,

148

but only as to whether same is in violation of the law.

'The people must establish that the defendants are guilty of violation of Section 1141 beyond a reasonable doubt. After a careful reading of the entire book, we conclude that the book in question is not in violation of the law.'

It seems strange that in her biography of Radclyffe Hall, Una Troubridge failed to record this remarkable legal triumph, or to give credit for it to the firm which was indubitably responsible. Perhaps by that time the two women were both weary of *The Well of Loneliness,* or perhaps did not regard American newspapers as worthy of much attention. At any rate, it was left to another American publication, *The International Journal of Sexology,* published by the University of Indiana, to draw some legitimate conclusions in an article on *The Personality of Radclyffe Hall* by Dr Clifford Allen.

'The time has come when the judges should try to interpret the spirit and not the letter of the law and realise that what the legislators meant by obscene was an attempt to corrupt. If a book presents abnormality in such a way as to entice the innocent into trying some practice likely to harm them, then that is obscene; if not, if it presents only the truth, then it is not obscene to normal minds. If we use this criterion, which is the only sensible one, with regard to a book like Radclyffe Hall's *The Well of Loneliness,* how far is it obscene? Does it describe homosexual practices so that young, pure, innocent girls are likely to feel a longing to try them? It does nothing of

149

the sort. On the contrary it shows the unhappiness, the misery, the long drawn-out search of an abnormal woman, to find a modicum of joy.

'Like all Radclyffe Hall's books it is basically honest. She may have had faults in style, she undoubtedly fell occasionally from the novelist's detachment and indulged in sentimentality with regard to her characters, but on no occasion did she indulge in dishonesty, nor did she describe things falsely or cast a gloss over what was real. She never pretended that homosexuality led to other than unhappiness. It was her honesty which caused her books being banned . . .

'It is mainly owing to Radclyffe Hall's stand that public opinion has accepted a widening of the novelist's range and a less hypocritical attitude has been taken regarding things which everybody knows exist. It is doubtful whether posterity will place her in the first rank but now that she is dead it is easier to put her in a true perspective. Her true position is that of an honest writer and not as a purveyor of dirty books.'

This was confirmed by the reception accorded the book by the American press, which was commendatory and enthusiastic.

*   *   *

New York Herald Tribune
The Well of Loneliness is much more of a sermon than a story, a passionate plea for the world's under-

150

standing and sympathy, as much a novel of problem and purpose as *Uncle Tom's Cabin,* as sentimental and moralistic as the deepest-dyed of the Victorians ... *The Well of Loneliness* is courageous and honest ... Perhaps her (Miss Hall's) book will facilitate public discussion of the subject by dispassionate scientists; certainly suppression of the novel would contribute to still further public misunderstanding.

*   *   *

Brooklyn Daily Eagle
At any rate, there doesn't seem to be anything in the American edition to cause Mr Sumner and his keepers of the public conscience to break in upon their holiday shopping for the purpose of driving sin from our doorsteps ... the author is found guilty of a certain desperate earnestness which completely eliminates the novel from the luridly sensational.

*   *   *

Philadelphia Inquirer
The Well of Loneliness is not only remarkably fine literature, which demands slow, careful reading, but is a serious, repressed study of a subject which must always remain a tragedy ...

*   *   *

Philadelphia Public Ledger
The book is a human document, written, I think, with deep gravity of purpose. So far as I have been able to detect, the book was not planned with any ulterior motive to achieve sensation ... naughtiness can be

151

found much more easily in twenty novels, recently published, I might name ... Miss Hall has written with delicacy, with careful anxiety not to offend the reader. In this respect alone, Miss Hall has achieved no little. And of course she achieved something more. As a tract, as case history, as a document reporting with sincerity the tragic condition of a very special mental and physical aberration . . . *The Well of Loneliness* is a book which may not be ignored.

Walter Yust

*   *   *

The Nation
It is the opinion of *The Nation* (1) that Radclyffe Hall's book deals in an intelligent, unsensational, and entirely proper way with the unhappy life of a woman struggling against perverse tendencies and is well worth while to call public attention to the badly misunderstood plight of many, many men and women; (2) that any attempt to declare any subject of human interest and social significance as *per se* undiscussable is not only to further confuse the already difficult subject of criminal obscenity, but also to promote a socially dangerous obscurantism.

*   *   *

The New Republic
...*The Well of Loneliness* is a novel of unusual power, distinction and charm, thoroughly English in quality.

Robert Morse Lovett

152

8

AFTERMATH

IMMEDIATELY THE loss of the Appeal in England became known, a number of prominent writers organised a round robin protesting against the suppression of a book with genuine literary qualities.

This effort, as might have been expected at that date, did not succeed in its purpose. *The Well of Loneliness* remained a suppressed publication in England until vindicated much later in the law courts. It was, however, obtainable in the U.S.A. and in Paris, where a second-rate dramatisation attracted a number of foreign travellers.

Thirty years later, when the law had been amended to allow evidence of literary merit to be given in obscenity cases, Lord Birkett gave his own final judgment.

'I was counsel for the defence of the book and had perforce to read it with a most critical eye, keeping in mind at all times the wording of the Act of Parliament. I felt then, and feel now, that there was no word of obscenity in that book from the first to the last, and that to call it an obscene publication was a dreadful misuse of language. Sir Chartres Biron condemned the book because it described a certain relationship between women, and Miss Radclyffe Hall, who wrote the book, had not stigmatised this relationship as being in any way blameworthy ...

'It is an indication of the world of rapid change in which we live, and of the vagaries of taste, that *The Well of Loneliness* is now on sale in every bookshop without the slightest interference from the police or the Director of Public Prosecutions or anybody else. The phials of prussic acid can be taken freely without apparent injury to the citizen or the State.'*

Even today, Corgi Books have announced that they are publishing a paper-back edition to meet the obvious demand in this country, which is due to come out in August 1968, while an up-to-date record of the foreign sales, supplied by Messrs A. M. Heath & Co. Ltd, gives their total (in 14 languages) as 551,910 copies.

In America the book was published first by Alfred Knopf and later by Garden City Books, which still

---

* Quoted from C. H. Rolph, *Does Pornography Matter* (1961), pp. 2–3, and also from H. Montgomery Hyde, *Norman Birkett. The Life of Lord Birkett of Ulverton,* pp. 259–60.

154

has an edition in print. It was issued in the United States without expurgation and continues to have a considerable sale.

When Radclyffe Hall died in 1943, *The Times* obituary notice said of her: 'Radclyffe Hall had abundant sympathy and pity, and views on her controversial book should not be allowed to rob her of credit for her sterling literary qualities, her well-controlled emotional pitch, her admirable prose style.'

It also gave the value of her estate as £118,015, all bequeathed to Una Troubridge, who was directed to destroy her friend's last book. Radclyffe Hall, being a well-to-do woman in her own right, only a small proportion of this substantial estate came from the foreign sales of *The Well of Loneliness*.

Una Troubridge left no direct family, her only daughter having been killed not long after her own death, in a car accident in 1966. As Una died in Italy, where she went to live after the Second World War ended, some of the minor directions of Radclyffe Hall's will could not be carried out.

Eventually *The Well of Loneliness* case had widespread legal and social effects, from which the defendants in the case of *Lady Chatterley's Lover* (1960) clearly benefited. More doubtful, though still debatable, is the possible effect upon Radclyffe Hall herself. Can her last illness, fifteen years after the Appeal failed, possibly be traced to the obloquy and abuse she endured, which must have been extremely painful to a sensitive author even though she deliberately invited it?

So little is known even now about the interaction of mind and body that the inoperable cancer from which Radclyffe Hall died, twenty years before the death of her friend and lover, may well have been indirectly related to the anguish of mind which *The Well of Loneliness* hearing must have caused her. A general connection between cancer and mental suffering does appear to have been established and accepted by certain doctors.

The legal effects of *The Well of Loneliness* case are more evident and less susceptible to argument. Recent laws on obscenity, for example, the Obscene Publications Act of 1959 and 1964, and the closely related Children and Young Persons (Harmful Publications) Act clearly distinguish between sin and crime. Section 4 of the Act of 1959, under the general heading 'Defence of Public Good' recognises the validity of the ruling of Sir Chartres Biron that the opinion of experts was not evidence, but introduced a clause making it possible for the first time.*

At the hearing of the case against *Lady Chatterley's Lover* (October 20th, 1960), thirty-five distinguished men and women of letters and other relevant professions were called to give evidence, while at least as many held themselves in readiness to appear. In contrast to the contemptuous dismissal (in under ten minutes) of Radclyffe Hall's appeal in 1928, the prosecution of D. H. Lawrence's book (the first to be

---

* A person shall not be convicted of an offence against section two of this Act, and an order for forfeiture shall not be made under the foregoing section, if it is proved that publication of the article in question is justified as being for the public good on the ground that it is in the interests of science, literature, art or learning, or of other objects of general concern...'

'It is hereby declared that the opinion of experts as to the literary, artistic, scientific or other merits of an article may be admitted in any proceedings under this Act either to establish or to negative the said ground.'

Obscene Publications Act 1959,
Section 4 (1) & (2).

prosecuted under the Act of 1959), resulted in a unanimous verdict of 'Not Guilty' which was received with an outburst of clapping. This verdict, says the jacket description of the Penguin Edition of *The Trial of Lady Chatterley* in 1962, 'was a shock, mainly one of pleasure and relief, to lovers both of English literature and moral sanity. For it was not just a legal tussle, but a conflict of generation and class.'

Assuming no violent reactionary change of opinion, which would be contrary to the experience of history, the legal battle appears to have been finally won. Still at issue is the question how far homosexuality should be socially as well as legally accepted. But the whole trend, both of modern legislation and social practice in this field, is against the creation of moral pariahs.

A symbol of this change is perhaps the acceptance by the National Portrait Gallery of Charles Buchel's painting of Radclyffe Hall, offered to them in 1963 under the Will of Una Troubridge, to whom it was bequeathed. Today this picture can be seen on request without difficulty of any kind. By giving her a position among those worthy to be remembered by their country, the Establishment reversed the moral judgment passed on its subject by a censorious public forty years earlier, and offered her, in effect, a species of accolade.

In fact, modern society owes a debt to Radclyffe Hall. Her qualities of humour may have been limited, and less remarkable than her qualities of mercy, and an element of self-pity perhaps impaired her far-sighted compassion for the victims of 'God's Good People'. But she brought the individual practices falsely and cruelly labelled 'vice' out of the region of the furtive snigger, and the darkness of the hidden

157

places where the real obscenities of human life crawl under stones, into the light of day. Thus she conferred on her kind the benefit of full and free discussion which, though often critical, is at least an honest recognition of a biological fact.

If the lesbian of today is regarded, not as a pariah whose eccentricities are a form of depravity, but as a part, if only a small part, of the human pattern, it is largely because Radclyffe Hall accepted crucifixion, and made her own story a factor in the growth of understanding and hence of toleration.

APPENDIX

BY RICHARD DU CANN

By 1928 the law relating to the common law misdemeanour of obscene libel had stood virtually unchanged for 200 years. It was in 1727 that the common law courts had first accepted that an act 'tending to corrupt the morals of the King's subjects' and 'destructive of morality in general, if it does, or may, affect the King's subjects' could make the author or disseminator liable to punishment.

It was not that such writings had been previously unknown. In 1668 Samuel Pepys recorded his feeling of shame for allowing himself to read *L'escholle des filles* at his booksellers, yet less than a month later he went back to buy a copy for himself 'in plain binding' (customs die hard in this trade) finding it a 'mighty lewd book'. Seven years later the Dean of All Souls at Oxford caught some of the gentlemen of the College apparently engaged in printing *Aretine's Postures* ('Twenty plates showing all the various ways, attitudes and positions in which licentious men have intercourse with women . . . and for each plate . . . an indecent sonnet') on the College press, and there are a number of recorded prosecutions for publishing such diverse works as *The Wandering Whore* and *The Whore's Rhetorick.*

But such publications were either dealt with in the ecclesiastical courts or their content was such that they could be said to be libelling some religious or political or social group, so that the word 'libel' in the offence had some real meaning, and the word 'obscene' simply described the type of libel. Faced in 1708 with James Read and Angell Carter's publication *Fifteen Plagues of a Maidenhead* which was plain pornography unadulterated by any extraneous material (the title faithfully anticipates the contents), the common law courts had refused to record a conviction, Chief Justice Holt accurately observing: 'This does not libel anyone.' He added, with even more accuracy: 'They do it simply to make money.'

But in 1727, despite the protests of Mr Justice Fortescue who thought the courts should have nothing to do with the Attorney-General's devious argument to induce the courts to fashion a new offence, the same court confirmed the Indictment against a man named Curl who had published in English the French classic *Venus in the Cloister or the Nun in her Smock.* This abrupt about-face could be explained by the religious denigration implicit in the text which is broadly a dialogue between two nuns as to the sexual experiences to be tasted within holy orders but without their smocks, but the judgment of

160

the court does not appear to rely on that for its justification.

As a result the crime of obscene libel, having nothing to do with libel in its generally understood sense, was established. By the time *The Memoirs of a Woman of Pleasure,* better known simply as *Fanny Hill* was published in 1749, John Cleland and the printers and publishers did not attempt to challenge the legal basis of the warrant on which they were arrested. Thereafter any distinction between an obscene libel, which in fact libelled some person or group of persons, and one which libelled no one but was simply obscene, was a distinction without a difference. Both were obscene libels and as such liable to prosecution before a jury as a common law (i.e. Judge-made and not statute-made) misdemeanour.

But prosecution before a jury, or on Indictment as it is called, is slow, cumbrous and expensive, and at that time was also extremely uncertain. The Indictment had to set out the passages complained of; the smallest error and the Indictment was liable to be quashed for there was no means of amending it. Those concerned with and for the moral welfare of the country knew that prosecutions were often not brought when they ought to have been and that prosecutions had failed when they ought not to have done. At the same time, as the Nineteenth Century advanced, the willingness of the legislature to interfere in the activities of others on the grounds of what can loosely be called 'public conscience' increased considerably and the demands of the moralists for a quick and easy means to prevent the dissemination of obscene literature received a ready hearing. The result was Lord Campbell's Act of 1857. This has been widely misunderstood. It made no alteration to the definition of the offence, but merely made the suppression of what was considered morally undesirable very much easier.

The Preamble to the Act recites that it is an Act '... for more effectively preventing the sale of obscene books, etc. ...' and it goes on to claim '... that it is expedient to give additional powers for the suppression of the trade in obscene books, etc. ...' The Act gave Justices of the Peace power to issue search warrants and thereafter to order the destruction of any material '... of such a character and description that publication of them would be a misdemeanour' (i.e. if they were an obscene libel).

Between the seizure of the books found when the search warrant was executed, and the Justices' destruction order, there was to be no trial save that when the seized material was put before the Justices (if they were satisfied that it was obscene), they were obliged to issue a summons calling on the occupier of the premises from which it was seized, or on the owner of the material, if he was known, requiring him 'to show cause why the articles so seized should not be destroyed'. Since it was only if the Justices were satisfied that the material was obscene that such a summons was issued, it was generally felt there was no conceivable purpose in seeking to show in public that they had been wrong in private, and Justices were able to make destruction orders without the trouble of a court hearing.

A more expeditious method of seizing and destroying books could hardly have been devised. It became law without a division in either the Lords or the Commons. Nine years later, in 1868, the decision in Hicklin's case made the Act apply with even greater force. In that case the Appeal Court defined as

162

obscene any article whose tendency was '. . . to deprave and corrupt those whose minds are open to such immoral influences and into whose hands a publication of this sort may fall'. Any book or picture having such a tendency was thereafter liable to prosecution on Indictment, where the standard of judgment would be that of a jury, or liable to seizure, where the standard of judgment would be that of local justices or a stipendiary magistrate. The Chief Justice also stated his own view of the book in the case, making it clear how he thought the test ought to be applied. The book was certain, he said, '. . . to suggest to the minds of the young of either sex, or even persons of more advanced years, thoughts of a most impure and libidinous character'.

It is easy to scoff at these words today, but thoughts of a 'libidinous character' are cultivated by advertising techniques until the stimulus, if not the reaction to that stimulus, has become a commonplace of daily life. Then, and for ninety years afterwards, the idea behind the words – that the public dissemination of works dealing in sexual matters or with a sexual theme aroused a sexual response, and that that response was morally reprehensible – dominated the decisions in this field. As a result, a host of books was destroyed and reputations of an army of authors tarnished, of whom Radclyffe Hall was only one. Charles Bradlaugh and Annie Besant, George Moore, Thomas Hardy and Ibsen all suffered in the nineteenth century at the hands of those holding this view; H. G. Wells, D. H. Lawrence, James Joyce and Bernard Shaw in the twentieth. As time went on, the position of the author became if anything worse, for while social restrictions on the freedom with which he could explore explicit sexual situations were removed, the legal rules, formulated since 1727 and 1868, remained and were enforced.

As a result one finds concentrated in the proceedings against *The Well of Loneliness* all that special injustice which only the grinding machinery of justice can bring. By 1928 Lord Campbell's Act, under which these proceedings were brought, had not been amended, so that Radclyffe Hall, being neither the occupier of the premises from which the books were seized nor the owner of those books, had no right of audience, although it was her book upon which judgment was to be given. Furthermore, any one passage in the book, indeed one word, which could be judged obscene, was enough to condemn the whole book; it did not have to be read as a whole, and in deciding the question of obscenity the intention of the author and the literary merit of the work were irrelevant, save that again and again it had been successfully argued that the better written the book, the more serious the libel. Lastly, as a result of the Hicklin test fifty years before, the standard by which *The Well of Loneliness* was judged was that of the curious child, not that of the reasonable adult.

Radclyffe Hall suffered from all these deficiencies in the law. She suffered in full, for it is plain that Norman Birkett's handling of the case did not meet with her approval. What he said initially about the theme and purpose of the book may have pleased the publishers from whom he derived his instructions. It clearly did not please her. The change of direction he was forced to make half way through presenting the defence, after she had attacked him during the lunch interval, may have mollified her feelings but cannot have but done the defence a great deal of harm. In fact his handling of the whole case was despairingly unsubtle, the attempt to call evidence being particularly disastrous. After calling Desmond MacCarthy, who was probably the foremost literary critic of the day, to give evidence, Birkett asked the question: 'In your view is it (the book) obscene?' The magistrate would not allow MacCarthy to answer. Whatever view may be taken of Sir Chartres Biron's behaviour during the hearing or of his decision on the book, he could not have taken any other course about this part of the case. Whether the book was obscene or not was the very issue he had to try. He was bound to stop any witness giving evidence which in effect usurped or sought to usurp his own function. His intervention was inevitable. It must have been known by Birkett to be inevitable, yet Birkett did not ask MacCarthy any further questions and, having gone baldheaded into this irretrievable position, he did not tender any of his further thirty-nine witnesses on any other ground than this single objectionable one. But all of them could have said much more and, given the opportunity, would have said much more. They were never given the opportunity and the result was inevitable.

My own untutored guess is that Cape's lawyers thought Cape's actions long before the case began had created for them an impossible situation. Following Douglas' denunciation the publishers had sent a copy of the book to the Home Office for their opinion. The Home Office had said that the book ought to be withdrawn. Cape ostensibly bowed to that advice and ceased printing and distributing the book in England but handed the printing moulds over to the Pegasus Press in Paris. Birkett was therefore on slippery ground, for Cape had not chosen to stand and fight. He had outwardly accepted that the book was obscene, thereby reducing the risk of prosecution in this country, while privately arranging for publication abroad. Birkett's argument that the book was not obscene was hoist on Cape's petard. If the public in and out of court did not realise this, Sir Chartres Biron did; his comment on the failure of Cape to give evidence was clearly referring to it. The further evidence called by the prosecution on the hearing of the Appeal made the position even worse. After receiving the advice of the Home Office and sending the moulds to Paris, Cape instructed them: 'Please destroy any proofs you may have of the Paris title page. Cape's do not want it to be known the type has gone abroad.'

There was no way Birkett at Bow Street or Melville on the Appeal at the London Sessions could avoid the handicap created for them by the publishers. If Birkett, with Rubinstein, Melville, Metcalfe and Frampton, a formidable array of legal minds, could find no way out of the strait-jacket imposed by the common law and statute in the period of two hundred years before 1928, it was unlikely that any other lawyer could. So it proved, and it was not until the Obscene Publications Act of 1959 that the conditions which had proved to be so intolerable for more than a hundred years of that time were ameliorated. But, by one of those curious contradictions, it was a lawyer who gave the impetus needed to induce concerted action which finally brought about a change in the law.

In the nineteen-fifties there was a spate of prosecutions at the Old Bailey against the publication of a number of modern novels. One of these was *The Philanderer,* published by Secker & Warburg in 1955. By chance the Judge was Mr Justice Stable whose summing-up to the jury was a revelation. He told them what ought to be the object of any legislation dealing with obscenity: 'I do not suppose there is a decent man or woman in this court who does not wholeheartedly believe that pornography, filthy books, ought to be stamped out and suppressed. They are not literature. They have got no message; they have got no inspiration; they have got no thought. They have got nothing. They are just filth, and ought to be stamped out'. And he pointed the danger of applying the Hicklin standard too literally: 'Are we to take our literary standards as being the level of something that is suitable for the decently brought up young female of fourteen? ... Of course not. A great mass of literature, from all angles, is wholly unsuitable for reading by the adolescent, but that does not mean that a publisher is guilty of a criminal offence for making those works available to the general public.'

It was the first ray of light in a hitherto exclusively dark and unfriendly world. But translating these words into practical legal terms was not easy and, although the Act of 1959 accomplished its main task, the Act had to be amended within five years to cure it of two major errors. The most substantial injustices, however, were all removed. The common law offence was abolished and replaced by the statutory offence of publishing an obscene article. The Act requires that the article should be read as a whole, and its tendency to deprave and corrupt tested in relation to those persons '... who, having regard to all the relevant circumstances ...' were likely to '... read, see or hear the matter contained or embodied in it'. This meant that at last the test of the innocent schoolgirl who happened to see one page was abolished.

By Section 4 a defence of 'public good' was created, so that if it was proved that the publication of an article which was obscene was justified as being for the public good on the grounds 'that it is in the interests of science, literature, art or learning, or other objects of general concern', then no conviction would follow. The Act further declared that the opinion of experts was admissible to establish or negative those grounds. The Act did not abolish the Lord Campbell procedure. Instead it simplified it, but it also gave the right to the 'owner, author or maker' of the seized article, or 'any person through whose hands the article had passed' to be heard on any proceedings for forfeiture.

One of the stated objects of the Act was the protection of literature. In this direction the Act has been only partially successful, for there have been undoubted mistakes in applying the Act, and there was one bone of contention which was not put right until some years later. The Act does not specify how or when one procedure for dealing with allegedly obscene material or another should be chosen.

In 1963 *The Memoirs of a Woman of Pleasure* was seized by the Metropolitan police and taken before the Chief Magistrate sitting at Bow Street. Further copies were seized from the printers in Manchester and taken before the Justices sitting there. Despite protests from the publishers that they wanted a verdict from a jury, the proceedings were continued before these local courts.

The same action was taken, again despite protests, when *Cain's Book* by Alexander Trocchi was seized by the police in Sheffield. Subsequently the Attorney-General gave an undertaking in the House of Commons that, in any future case in which it was claimed an article had merits which might afford a defence of 'public good', opportunity would be given for that to be tested by a jury. Another deficiency liable to lead to a lack of conformity in the application of the Act was put right when Section 25 of the Criminal Justice Act 1967 became law. This prevented civilian vigilantes from obtaining search warrants under the Act to seize books which they considered to be obscene, even after the Director of Public Prosecutions or their local police force had decided that no action should be taken.

Since 1959 the working of the Act has been tested in the courts in a number of cases. Three of these are of outstanding importance. The first and best known was the trial of Penguin Books Limited for their publication in 1960 of *Lady Chatterley's Lover*. Few recent trials have aroused greater interest, even fewer have been more misrepresented. So much has been written about the case by those who knew little of the detail, possibly less about literature and undoubtedly nothing of the law and procedure involved, that it is perhaps not surprising that the significance of some important aspects of the case has been substantially obscured by dust raised through the grinding of personal axes.

Quite apart from the result of the case and the realisation that a serious work of literature could be protected, in two respects the case advanced the limits of the law to a point where for the first time such a work could be properly examined. Neither decision attracted attention at the time and little has been paid to them since, yet if either had existed in 1928 Radclyffe Hall would have had no complaint. Both came on the second day of the trial, when witnesses being called for the defence continually sought to

169

offer their opinion that the book was not obscene. This is no more permissible now than in 1928 for the reason which has already been stated. Others sought to say virtually the same thing but in a different way – that Lawrence did not *intend* that the book should be obscene, adding that he was a writer with great integrity of purpose.

In some countries, particularly America, the test of intention – is it 'dirt for dirt's sake'? – decides the issue of obscenity by itself. Had Mr Justice Byrne so ruled, he would have been flouting the words of the Act of Parliament. What he did say was that the author's intention, so far as testing obscenity was concerned, was irrelevant, but 'as far as literary merit or other matters that can be considered under Section 4 (the defence of public good), one has to have regard to what the author was trying to do, what his message may have been and what his general scope was'. Even with the limitation that the author's intention must be 'as shown by the book', and not by the author's other writings, in the history of the trials of allegedly obscene writing this decision was little short of revolutionary, for it immediately removed one of the final injustices under which the author smarted.

Within an hour of that decision the Judge also ruled that 'any judgment of the literary and other merits of a book is one necessarily involving comparisons', and that 'the literary merit of this book can be dealt with by comparing it with the literary merit *or otherwise* of other books'. Prior to the passing of the 1959 Act, the courts had ruled that direct comparisons between the book complained of and other books which circulated freely, were not permitted on the basis that the court was solely concerned with the book before it and with no others. It now became possible, without making a direct comparison with any named book, to evaluate the literary merit of the book on trial by comparing it both with well-written books, and with the whole stream of badly written and pornographic material available in this country.

So, following the Act and the amendments and the trial of *Lady Chatterley,* a book could be judged as a whole and not in part; it could be judged not merely on the words employed but also on its honesty of purpose; and it could be judged by the public at large in the climate of that day's standards. This did not mean that the author, printer and publisher could look forward to a roseate future free from the policeman's gaze. The boundary between what is and what is not permissible is not a fixed and unwavering one. It may well vary from place to place and certainly from time to time. Mistakes will be made. Some it is claimed already have been. One is said to involve the second important trial since 1959; *Cain's Book,* seized by the Sheffield police in 1964.

The publishers intervened in the proceedings to show cause why the book should not be forfeit and sought to show by the evidence of five expert witnesses that the literary and sociological merits outweighed the obscenity, if any, of the book. No witnesses were called by the prosecution to rebut this evidence, but nevertheless the Justices rejected it and made their order for forfeiture. (As had the Magistrate at Bow Street and the Justices in Manchester in similar proceedings against *Fanny Hill,* also although no rebuttal evidence had been called by the prosecution.)

On appeal the Lord Chief Justice said that the Justices were entitled to take this course, for it was for them to weigh the merits of the book against the obscenity and to decide if the publication was for the public good. Although superficially illogical, this is clearly correct for the question of public good, like that of obscenity, is not one about which evidence can be given and must be for the court to decide. But the further argument was put forward that the finding of the Justices that the book was obscene was not based on the tendency to deprave or corrupt sexually, but on the basis that readers might be induced to experiment with drugs, the theme of the book being concerned with drug addiction. The Court held that there was '... no reason whatever to confine the Act to sex'. This ruling, which runs directly counter to the law on obscene publications since 1727 – in the sense that there never has been any case of obscenity which was not primarily concerned with explicitly sexual matters – has had, and will continue to have, far-reaching consequences.

One of these, the third trial of importance since 1959, occurred in 1966 when a company was prosecuted for publishing cards inserted in packets of bubble-gum and sold to children of five years old and upwards. The cards showed 'battle scenes' of the Second World War, of which it was said that the violence tended to deprave and corrupt the children who would buy them. In support of this view, the prosecution sought to call medical evidence to show what effect the pictures would have on the children who might buy them. The Justices refused to hear the evidence, but the Appeal Court ruled that they should, provided the evidence was limited to what effect the cards would have on a child, and what they would cause a child to do, and that the direct question: 'Is that a sign of corruption or depravity?' was not asked.

This is the sort of hair splitting which is commonly

thought to delight a lawyer but is the despair of the layman. On this occasion the layman may be right, for if witnesses may not speak as to whether an article is obscene or not, how can they be permitted to give evidence of the 'effect' which results only from the presumption of obscenity?

In the trial of *Last Exit to Brooklyn* at the Old Bailey in 1967, threads from all three of these cases could be plainly seen. From the *Lady Chatterley* trial the publishers forged the linch-pin of their defence: the integrity of the author and the modern climate of literature in which he wrote. From the appeals in *Cain's Book* and the bubble-gum case, the prosecution founded their attack: the repeated and excessive scenes of violence and drug taking as well as the emphasis on natural and unnatural sexual acts. From the bubble-gum case both sides took authority to ask their respective witnesses what effect the book had had on them, even though those witnesses were not medical experts. Some of the replies went far beyond what was contemplated even in that case. In the end the jury followed the example set by the Justices dealing with *Cain's Book* and *Fanny Hill* by appearing to reject the expert evidence called by the defence, and convicted.

As a result, those who are devoted to the cause for the abolition of all censorship maintain that the faster we move forward the more we stay in the same place. This is patently inaccurate so far as publications are dealt with under the old common law misdemeanour and now under the 1959 Act. However, it may be true of a variety of other Acts dealing with public behaviour. *Lady Chatterley's Lover* may circulate freely at paperback price, but take out one of the four letter words and put it on an advertising hoarding, and without doubt an offence contrary to the Indecent Advertisements Act of 1889 would be alleged against the persons responsible. Similarly, a performance of one of the acts of sexual intercourse described in the book in a public place would, quite apart from any local bye-law, cause those involved to be liable to be convicted under the Vagrancy Act of 1824.

Few people would argue that this is wrong. What is suitable for private enjoyment is not by any means suitable for public display. Lawyers would be the first to agree, however, that much of this legislation needs a drastic overhaul. Section 28 of the Town Police Clauses Act of 1847, for instance, makes it an offence to display a 'profane or indecent or obscene book', or to sing a 'profane or obscene song or ballad', or to use any 'profane or obscene language'. Provided therefore your songs, ballads and language are only indecent, and not obscene or profane, you can escape conviction.

If the study of the old statutes is not very profitable, it is frequently very entertaining. Those in this field provide the usual crop of discrepancies and anomalies, none of which is really important. But two Acts of Parliament maintain penal provisions which are largely unknown and upon any view are logically unjustifiable, for they impose on literature and art a double standard. Section 42 of the Customs Consolidation Act 1876 authorises the Customs and Excise to seize any 'indecent or obscene' articles on their importation into this country. If the articles are imported 'fraudulently', which probably means no more than deliberately, and with intent to evade the prohibition on their importation, then a maximum sentence of two years' imprisonment can be passed.

Section 11 of the Post Office Act 1952, which

repeats an earlier Act in identical terms, prohibits the sending of any 'obscene or indecent' article through the post. A maximum sentence of twelve months imprisonment is prescribed. A decision of the Court of Criminal Appeal in 1965 shows that in these two Acts and the others referred to earlier, which use these two words in the form 'indecent or obscene', the words cover a far wider field than is covered by the words 'obscene articles' in the Obscene Publications Acts. In that year the Lord Chief Justice approved the definition of indecent as 'something that offends the ordinary modesty of the ordinary man'. He stated: 'The words "indecent" and "obscene" convey one idea, namely offending against the recognised standard of propriety, indecent being at the lower end of the scale and obscene at the upper end of the scale.'

Lawyers are frequently blamed for seeking to define the indefinable. In fact it is generally the hasty imprecision of the politician rather than the fussy meticulousness of the lawyer which drives them to do so. This is a classic example which misfired, for the truth is that obscenity has nothing to do with standards of propriety, recognised or otherwise, and everything to do with corruption and depravity. If the struggle to introduce a sensible and workable system by which written and printed matter can properly be judged has achieved anything at all, it should mean that taste, or the ordinary modesty of the ordinary man, is wholly irrelevant. This seems to me to have particular importance when it is remembered that, as the law stands, works can be freely offered for sale in this country which are not obscene, which can be read and studied by the public at their own discretion, but which if imported or sent through the post could, solely on the grounds of their offensiveness to that recognised standard, make the importer and sender liable to penalties in a criminal court. Such works, of course, are in exactly the same position in relation to a charge of indecency, as all works were before the Obscene Publications Act in relation to a charge of obscenity: they do not have to be read as a whole, the integrity and intention of their producer is irrelevant, and no defence of 'public good' can be advanced.

Since neither the Customs and Excise nor the Post Office need to retain these powers in order to preserve their efficient operation, nor do the public at large require their retention in order that they may be properly protected, the actual retention of them may be thought to be unjustified. It simply leads to the ridiculous sort of situation typified by the case cited from in 1965 where, if the producer of strip-tease films had distributed his wares over the counter instead of sending them through the post, he would not have been convicted, for the jury who tried him acquitted him of publishing obscene material and only convicted him of sending indecent articles through the post. The law can do without this patent absurdity. So can the public.

The public also needs to think very carefully before permitting lawyers to embark on a development of the ideas implicit in the *Cain's Book* and bubble-gum cases. As these decisions stand at present, they can be extended so as to allow the courts to intervene in areas in which they have hitherto refused to trespass and in a manner they have refrained from adopting. Current moral opinion, at the social and intellectual level of the courts, might make intervention by the courts seem desirable, but this is a short term view. It might be right to say that a man can be depraved and

176

corrupted in relation to drugs or violence, as well as in relation to sex, even though the courts have never said so during the last three hundred years. Is it right that the courts should go further and say that a man can be corrupted and depraved in relation to racial prejudice or political intolerance? A man can obviously be so corrupted, but who should take steps to prevent it?

Parliament is subject to the scrutiny of the public. The courts are not. The Judges who decided the Appeal in the bubble-gum case may be right in saying that, faced with the issues raised on a prosecution for 'corruption and depravity', the courts, to quote from one judgment, 'need all the help they can get' from all classes of persons who can be called as witnesses, but if those witnesses are to be allowed to give evidence of opinion as to the effects of writings dealing with sex, drugs and violence, then why should they not give similar evidence on racial or political matters?

Little thought has at present been given to these problems: much needs to be. In an age when the common law needed to perform the functions also of the legislature, simply because there was no effective legislature, it was clearly right that lawyers should encourage the courts to act in areas where action was necessary, and that the public should applaud them when they did so. This is not true today. The popularity of the cry 'lawyer heal thyself', should not be taken by the lawyer as implying that he should attempt to heal others not yet subject to his jurisdiction. The view of the lawyer is too narrow, his life too confined by precedent and his immersion in the exact facts of the case too deep, for him to be able to take time or opportunity to examine the implications of

177

decision he may make in fields where he has not previously wandered.

Leaving it to the political arm of society may seem to many jumping out of the frying pan in order only to add to the fire. (After all, it took fifty years of continual pressure to achieve the Act of 1959, which required an amending Act only five years later, an undertaking by the Attorney-General in the House of Commons and a further provision in yet another Act, before it began to operate efficiently.) But undermining of the gains made by the Act through an extension of the ideas set out in the preceding paragraph, must be resisted before they impose a closer control than existed formerly.

Some may welcome that control. Most will not. All will agree that nothing needs to be resisted more than the activities of those who seek, under the guise of the freedom which the 1959 Act has brought, to peddle just that kind of filth to which Mr Justice Stable referred so exactly: '... they have got no message; they have got no inspiration; they have got no thought. They have got nothing. They are just filth.'

It is from the debasement of words and pictures by articles which fall into this category that the greatest danger lies for the future. The beauty of man's passion is defiled and the status of man himself degraded by works which have no compassion but pretend great understanding of his more bizarre activities. They do nothing save inculcate at best an individual and future self-abuse, and at worst a widespread and permanent destruction of true values.

Richard du Cann.

Queen Elizabeth Building
Temple, E.C.4   *2nd January 1968*

178

INDEX

185